From Private to CEO
(And Some Stuff In Between)

John Petrie

Cumulus Publishing Co.
Fort Worth, Texas

Copyright © 2019 by John Petrie

All rights reserved.

Published in the United States by Cumulus Publishing Co., a division of In The Cloud Copy, Fort Worth, Texas.
www.inthecloudcopy.com

Cumulus Publishing Co. and its logo are property of In The Cloud Copy.

First publication run, 2019.

Names: Petrie, John.
Title: From Private to CEO (And Some Stuff In Between) / By John Petrie
Description: First edition. | Fort Worth, TX : Cumulus Publishing, 2019 | English
Identifiers: ISBN 978-1-951206-00-0 (print) | ISBN ISBN: 978-1-951206-01-7 (ebook)

Design by Kristi Waterworth Hemmann
Cover Design and Illustrations by Sara M. Barcus
Photos copyright © John Petrie

Dedication

This book, along with all my accomplishments, could not have been realized without my partner in life, my wife of 35 years, Claudia, who endured military life and the challenges of multiple transitions in civilian life and kept me focused on becoming who I am today. I will love you always.

To my three wonderful daughters, Heather, Nicole, and Stacey, for bringing so much joy into my life.

To my parents for allowing me to make mistakes but learn from those mistakes and for the unconditional love that they gave me – it made me a better man.

To my brother, Gunnery Sergeant Joseph E. Petrie, United States Marine Corps (retired) (deceased), who was always competitive, kept me on my toes, and made me better at everything I did. I think of you every day.

To Captain Michael F. King, United States Marine Corps (deceased), for his friendship and direction and for teaching me about different cultures and the value of people. I will forever miss your counsel.

To Regina Polk Davis, a kindred spirit and friend who taught me about real friendship and is a role model for always striving to achieve even the hardest-to-reach dreams.

To Lieutenant Colonel Steve Sonnenberg, United States Marine Corps (retired), the consummate professional and gentleman who taught me that little things matter – a phone call, a note, a card – and to always show respect to women regardless of the situation. Things I continue to practice to this day.

To Frank Stafford, PhD, who guided me through the world of academia, the importance of education, and the world's need for research including the fundamentals of the 'business' of research.

To Charles Korbel for giving me an opportunity to be a security executive at a financial services organization, but as important, introducing me to the true meaning of quality and the leadership required to help your employees find success.

To Andrew Bland for being a consummate professional and demonstrating every day what it means to be a leader, a mentor, and a person who is a true friend.

To Steve Idelman for seeing beyond the individual and identifying the true potential and future value of a person. Thank you for giving me the chance to lead in my chosen field.

To Shinichi Yokohama for his trust and confidence in me over the years, his guidance, and his friendship. His collaboration and his thought leadership have been extremely valuable as I continue to evolve.

To Jun Sawada, I thank you for being a person of honor, a strong leader, a mentor, and an inspiration of what a true visionary is. You are a good man – and I am proud to have the opportunity to know you.

Contents

Dedication	**6**
Introduction	**10**
The Prequel	**12**
Chapter 1: Learning the Basics of Leadership	**13**

    The Initial Impact of Culture (1978-1979)
        Gathering Facts
        The Decision
        The Lessons Begin
        The Influence of Cultures
        The Far-East Experience

    Power Over Human Life (1980-1982)
        The Psychology of It All
        Molding the Human Spirit

    Life-Changing Experience – The Impact to Your View of the World (1983)
        Preparation
        The Battleground
        Reporters?
        Tragedy Strikes
        The Grasshopper
        The Fallout

    TWA Hijacking – The Algiers Operation (1985)

Chapter 2: Supporting the National Defense	**38**

    Panama – Learning Strategic Importance (1985-1989)
        The Core of Leadership
        The Canal
        Innovation Pays Off

    Decision-Making – The Impact on Lives (1990-1992)
        Supporting National Decision-Making
        No Room for Indecision
        Enhancing My Education

    The Calm of Kyoto (1992-1993)
        Meeting New Colleagues
        Meeting and Greeting
        To Understand Japan….

    Closing the Chapter – Retirement (1993-1996)
        The Next Duty Station
        Deploying Tech to the Field
        Reflecting on 20 Years of Service

Chapter 3: Starting Over – Reality of the Civilian World	**60**

    Defense Industrial Complex – Teaching
    Directed Energy Lab

- Diversified Personalities
- Proving a Negative
- Data Protection – The Early Experience

Consulting – Management Techniques

Chapter 4: CISO: Leading the Charge — 71
Management and Leadership, Two Different Things
- Adjusting Within Corporate Cultures
- Leveraging a Startup Culture

Expanding My Experience Base – CISO Development
- The First CISO Job
- Opportunity Knocks

International Exposure

Chapter 5: Managing Your Own Business — 83
The Challenge
Legalities
Independence

Chapter 6: The IBM Experience – Briefing Boards of Directors — 89
Big Blue in Action
The Idea
Looking Inside
Deflation of the Idea

Chapter 7: Global CISO – Things You Don't Learn from a Book — 96
Always Be Ready to Walk Through an Open Door
- Dinners Are Never Just Dinners

Negotiate! Everything's on the Table Until It's Not
- Always Be Prepared

A Regional Structure for a Global Company
- Restructuring and Growing Pains
- Strengths and Weaknesses

The Politics of It All
Continuing to Navigate the Changes

Chapter 8: CEO Was Never on the Bucket List — 107
More Challenges
- Managing Up
- Another Open Door
- Goals and Objectives that Are Clearly Articulated
- Know What You Are Worth
- The Puzzle Pieces
- The Picture

Continuing the Journey — 119
Leadership Lessons Over 40 Years — 120

Introduction

This book, by design, reflects my journey in my own professional life. Just as important to the story, though, are lessons I have learned through that process that I thought would be of interest to colleagues around the world. Multiple people have influenced me and provided guidance and suggestions that I have incorporated into my own leadership style. I hope to articulate those guiding principles throughout the book in a storytelling format.

I have made a concerted effort to give credit where credit is due, but in the interest of privacy I have used only initials of those people who have helped me along the way, unless I was able to get approval to use their name specifically. The list is long, and maybe that is the first point to make: you cannot do everything yourself, and you must learn to listen, engage with others, and collaborate.

Solutions to problems are almost always a collaborative effort. Successful leaders get input from multiple sources before a decision is made, but at the end of the day, good leaders make decisions. This leads me to two recurring themes throughout my journey: leadership is not the same as management, and indecision is a decision. These points will become very clear as the story unfolds. Planning is crucial in a personal journey, but even the best plans need to be reviewed and, perhaps, adjusted over time.

On September 10, 2018, I assumed my duties as the Chief Executive Officer (CEO) of NTT Security-Americas, a position and job that was never before on my radar screen. I will talk more about this in the book as a way to demonstrate that planning is crucial, self-assessment is crucial, and you must be positioned to walk through any open door as it is made available to you. Whether you choose to do so or not is strictly up to you.

The first or second question I get asked by my colleagues is how I went from a Global Chief Information Officer (GCISO) to a CEO. Apparently, this path is unique, and I will answer that question in detail. It is really more about how a person can prepare for an unforeseen opportunity rather than simply how I did what I did.

I start the description of this journey in October 1976, when I was just 17 years of age. This is where my introduction to discipline and leadership began. This path, of course, is certainly not recommended for everyone, but it is where my journey began, when an opportunity presented itself and I chose to walk through the door. Of course, that journey is still ongoing. I am positive that there will be other redirections on the path that will lead to additional opportunities, as well as the need for strategic decision-making along the way.

Time will tell.

My hope is that the guiding principles outlined in the story will be useful in your professional development and help you become a better leader.

Everybody matters! True leadership embodies that concept.

> *"Everyone wants to be better. Trust them.*
>
> *Leaders are everywhere. Find them.*
>
> *People achieve good things, big and small, every day. Celebrate them.*
>
> *Some people wish things were different. Listen to them.*
>
> *Everybody matters. Show them."*
>
> *– Bob Chapman, Chairman & CEO, Barry-Wehmiller*

The Prequel

In 1983, I was a Marine. I had left my home in Chicago for boot camp at Parris Island, South Carolina, in 1976, but I had never really understood what it meant to be a Marine at the core until I was face down in the soil, buried in the rubble of a makeshift bunker in the aftermath of a rocket attack.

Dirt filled my lungs, but with that last bit of adrenaline, I managed to push an arm up through the debris. As I lay there breathing that gritty air, knowing my death was imminent, I felt someone grab my hand and yank me out of my tomb.

I will forever be in that Corpsman's debt. And I will forever be in awe of the skills of our leadership that day, a day that's always fresh in my mind.

That was my defining moment. That was the day I understood what true leadership looked like, and it changed me irrevocably. It was the day I lived.

This book is full of moments that string together to make up a path to leadership – not THE path, understand, but a path, the one I took to reach the place where I am now.

Your path is your own, and there's no right way to gather the skills you'll need on your road. If you take nothing else from this book, I hope you'll keep this lesson: no matter where you are today, you can become a leader.

Chapter 1: Learning the Basics of Leadership

The Initial Impact of Culture (1978-1979)

Gathering Facts

When it comes to the choices we make in life and the steps it takes to get us there, there comes a point where two paths diverge. It's a small, maybe even insignificant, decision, but in retrospect, you can point to it and say, "There! That's it. That's when I started on this road."

> **Philosophical Statement Number One:**
> *You must be responsible and accountable for your decisions.*

It hadn't been long since I had dropped out of school (in the infinite wisdom of a teenager) and done my best to become a member of the Latin Kings, a notorious street gang active in the Chicago area at the time.

> **Philosophical Statement Number Two:**
> *You are never the sharpest tool in the shed – there is always someone smarter.*

My divergence came in September 1976. I had taken the over-500-mile trip to see my grandfather in Horseshoe Bend, Arkansas. There, as the leaves on the trees began to change colors, I asked my grandfather for his counsel. I had no idea what to do with my life, I explained, since school seemed useless and, with little work experience, my opportunities left me feeling impotent.

Much to my surprise, he poured us both a glass of bourbon and began to recount tales from his experiences in China during the war with Japan. He was a Navy man, one who was still proud of his time spent in service to his country.

> **Philosophical Statement Number Three:**
> *Always look to your elders for sage advice. Most of the time they have already been there, done that, and talks like that can save you a lot of time and provide a lot of good information.*

It wasn't long before he noticed how I was hanging on his every word, prompting an inserted caution with his stories. I wasn't to sign up for the military right away. This was a massive decision and not one to be rushed into. Yet, sensing my interest, my grandfather went on to explain the different benefits and drawbacks of each branch.

Not surprisingly, he placed the Navy among the top choices for young recruits, but he said the Marines was my best bet. After all, the Corps would teach me discipline and how to overcome any kind of obstacle, both real and imagined.

I was the last person who needed discipline, I told myself. He clearly didn't understand me.

I pushed back pretty hard.

The Decision

When I returned home, I told my parents that I'd made up my mind: I wanted to be a Marine. There was such an aura around the Marine Corps, even the recruiters were larger than life. That was who I wanted to be, where I belonged.

However, at 17, I wasn't old enough to join up without my parents' written consent. Luckily, my grandfather had prepared me for an uphill battle.

My parents were only half the equation, though. My girlfriend was also not thrilled with my announcement. It was a hard week, but as I was certain I was on the right path, I listened to and addressed each concern as it was presented to me.

> **Philosophical Statement Number Four:**
> *Consider all views, and weigh them accordingly, then own the decision.*

I laid out the pros and cons, much like my grandfather had done for me, hoping that my family would see how well I could fit into that culture. I knew I could get hurt, but hadn't I already been in danger year after year while wrestling and playing football in school?

My girlfriend protested that I could get killed, not just injured, but I was immovable. I was ready to go. They relented, and my parents signed the paperwork that allowed me to enlist in the Marines as my grandfather had suggested.

That fall was full of life-changing decisions. In late September, weeks before leaving for boot camp, I proposed to my girlfriend and she accepted.

The Lessons Begin

When a Marine recruit arrives at the training camp on Parris Island, South Carolina, they stand at attention on one of the many pairs of yellow boot prints painted on the pavement. Yes, THE infamous yellow footprints.

> **Philosophical Statement Number Five:**
> *There is always something worthwhile about a person; it is your job to find it.*

On that October day in 1976, they were the platform from which I launched my military career like so many Marines before me. There was nothing about that experience that I will ever forget. The drill instructors barked orders as they got all of the recruits into line. The intensity of that first taste of the Marine Corps was our introduction to the way Marines do discipline and order. It was both intimidating and very real.

I cannot stress the importance of my boot camp experience enough. The impression made upon me by one of my drill instructors, Sergeant J.M., is still relevant today. He taught me many things, including a lesson I've utilized and refined throughout my life: "don't let anyone tell you that you aren't good enough." He provided me with a foundation in leadership beyond the standard "respect, honor, and faithfulness" that was drilled into us on a daily basis.

With the help of Sergeant J.M. and many others, I was selected as the Honor Graduate for Platoon 3001, in January 1977. From there, we were all expected to apply everything we had learned in whatever position we held. I had entered the Marines under an open contract, meaning I could fill any position the Corps needed at the time. So, upon graduation, I sought further education in infantry training school at Camp Pendleton, California.

The training was difficult, but with a lot of effort I excelled and again graduated with honors as an 81mm mortar weapon specialist. I had my pick of duty stations and chose a military police posting at Marine Barracks, New London Submarine Base, Groton, New London, Connecticut.

There, I began a career in law enforcement and physical security. I was still a high school dropout, but I corrected that very poor decision while I was in New London, earning my diploma in October 1977. It was a great time for me. I even got to work with the Naval Investigative Service (NIS, now called NCIS) on several cases and rode in a diesel-powered submarine.

My grandfather had been right. The Marine Corps was the ideal solution for my young self, and honestly, it was really a great experience even this early in my service. My short stint as a military police Marine Guard gave me a chance to hone my people-reading skills, but it also taught me that all individuals deserve certain rights, regardless of the situation.

The Influence of Cultures

In late 1978, less than six months after my fiancée and I married and moved to our own apartment in New London, Connecticut, I was sent with a group of Marines to Norway for cold-weather training north of Oslo. There, we learned various skiing techniques and survival skills we would need should we end up in an arctic environment. Cold, after all, was the Norwegians' expertise, and they didn't hesitate to show us all they knew.

While there, we worked closely with people from all over the world – it was my first real exposure to other cultures. My friends in the British Royal Marines taught me the fine art of dry humor and regularly asked me how the colonies were doing.

It was a real eye-opener, one that helped me understand other people from their own perspectives for maybe the first time in my life. Certainly it was another opportunity for learning about how other people weren't really all that different.

Everything about that cold-weather training added to the base I was already working with and helped form my future as a leader.

Sadly, the sheer joy of the experience wasn't to last. When I landed in the States, I was met by my commanding officer, who immediately seized all of my weapons and demanded that I join him in his sedan. I knew it couldn't be good, as this was clearly not a normal welcome back from training.

Life Lesson:
Getting married at 18 was not such a good idea.

Lesson Learned:
Control your emotions and do not react to the moment – think through your decision.

I was blindsided when Major D. told me that my wife had moved out of our apartment and was staying with a friend. My first reaction was red, hot rage. I couldn't understand at the time what had happened; now I know that we were just too young and neither of us was really prepared for the realities of military life.

The Far-East Experience

Looking for a way to overcome the new turbulence in my life, I went back to work and was immediately returned to the rotating shift working as a Supervisor of Marines in Connecticut. Over the next few weeks, we had many minor dustups and increasingly started seeing small mobs of Iranian dissidents protesting at the gates. Although the protests were peaceful, tensions were rising, and we donned riot gear before reinforcing the barrier.

No one at our level of command could have

predicted what 1979 would have in store.

Things calmed again locally, with only minor incidents, while I learned various techniques for restraining men and women and honed my police skills. Having completed my initial time there at Marine Barracks, I requested assignment overseas.

I reported to the Third Battalion, Fourth Marine Regiment, Third Marine Division in Okinawa, Japan, in May 1979. I soaked in the culture, seized the opportunity to explore my new surroundings, and learned all I could about the Okinawans and the Japanese people when I wasn't on duty.

In Okinawa, I was immediately assigned to the Surveillance and Target Acquisition (STA) team and given a secondary position as an intelligence analyst working at the Third Battalion, Fourth Marines, S-2 shop – the military intelligence office for the unit. During my time with STA, I trained as a Scout Sniper. Learning to control my emotions, using both physical and mental exercises, was an extremely useful skill that helped me excel at both shooting and stealth movement.

I was promoted to Corporal in November 1979. Having multiple deployments as an Intelligence Analyst and Sniper under my belt including actions in the Philippines, Hong Kong, Thailand, Darwin, Australia, Singapore, and the Middle East, I had progressed rather quickly and was given additional responsibility. It wasn't unusual for me to be asked to conduct several jobs at the same time, serving both as a team leader and as a supervisor.

I was also dating an Okinawan nurse from the northern part of the island during this period. I had grown very fond of her and considered pursuing a deeper relationship.

As my time to move back to the States approached, I met with her parents, suggesting the idea of marriage (my Japanese was fair to good by that time). I was completely taken by surprise when they forbade their daughter to marry outside her race.

The young woman followed her parents' directive, and the relationship ended that evening. The cultural differences between Asia, the Middle East, America, and Europe were in many ways very contradictory, making multicultural interactions challenging for me at the time, though I continued to seek areas of commonality. The challenge would continue to shape my approach to others over the long term.

Power Over Human Life (1980-1982)

I was fortunate to have the chance at a young age to have many different types of experiences. They weren't all good and they weren't all bad, but I learned a lot from each one.

Life Lesson:
Stay away from gambling.

I had some leave (vacation) built up, so before heading back to California, I spent about 30 days traveling around Asia. I had been contemplating returning to civilian life, then I walked into a casino in Macau. Craps had been a familiar game in Chicago, but among the bright lights, loud noises, and massive excitement inherent in a casino, I lost myself – and my money.

The Psychology of It All

At 22, I had led Marines in combat situations, had pushed myself physically and mentally, and was working in a highly sensitive field. But, due to my mistakes in the casino during leave, instead of going into the private sector I reenlisted in July 1980, chose my next assignment, and moved back to San Diego, California.

There was a shortage of drill instructors at MCRD San Diego, giving me an opportunity to become one while only a Corporal – not typical practice at all. I was the only Corporal in the instructor education class. Few Marines are selected to become drill instructors, and fewer succeed. In short, it was a huge deal at the time, and I took advantage of it.

The course was intense. I went back to living as a recruit (so to speak) all over again, but in my mind, I was still "just" in San Diego, so it couldn't be that hard.

See, there are two types of Marines: Hollywood Marines, who do their recruit training in San

Diego, and Parris Island Marines, who go to Parris Island for recruit training. I can tell you from experience that the physical endurance and training are exactly the same. The mental anguish and challenges are different, but they are very present in both places.

In San Diego, you continuously see and hear the passenger planes taking off and landing from San Diego International Airport adjacent to MCRD. The noise is nonstop and enough to break down anybody's mental calm. Parris Island is exactly that, an island with no escape and sand fleas galore. There's nowhere to go if you decide you've made a huge mistake by enlisting.

The two bases are really more alike than they are different: the yellow footprints are the same, the barriers to leaving are still barriers, and you still have three drill instructors barking orders in your ears.

I was one of those nasty junior drill instructors that were called "devil dogs" by less than enthusiastic fans; those recruits only saw that we were mean and strictly by the book. Even though young Marines despised how we seemed to appear out of nowhere (obviously just to spy on them when they least expected us), everything we did was to help them succeed. The whole purpose of Marine recruit training is to break down each recruit to their viable base, then build them back up, train them, teach them and mature them into a fighting machine – a rifleman, a Marine.

Lesson Learned:
Identify shortcomings and try to improve them, but also build teams that rely on each other's strengths to counteract individual weaknesses

It may have seemed to my recruits like all I cared about was finding an excuse to pick on them, but the truth was that being part of one of the most unique training programs in the world was truly an honor and a privilege. I was molding boys into men every 13 weeks, controlling lives and mentoring fresh Marines. With this power comes a huge responsibility to also protect these individuals at their most vulnerable time while ensuring that they reach their potential.

Were there failures? Of course.

From 1980 to 1982, the attrition rate for San Diego MCRD was between 12 and 14% annually. In some cases, depending on the drill instructors involved, it could be as high as 25%.

The real work of drill instructors, myself included, was to weed out the individuals who could not make the transition into successful Marines. It is a simple formula. It's not about retaining potential soldiers; it's about making sure those who stayed would ultimately survive.

For the outcome to be a good one, I had to be better than the recruits – physically and mentally – and stay several steps ahead. But I always had the advantage because I knew when and how we would be breaking them down and bringing them back up.

Molding the Human Spirit

Being a drill instructor was the most rewarding experience of my life to that point and still is in the top five. I learned that you have to monitor yourself when you're trusted with so much power. Otherwise, it may corrupt you and destroy the people you manage. Having a good governance system, and in this case, a system of oversight, prevents a drill instructor or any leader from going too far.

Holding power over individuals is something that must be understood and carefully guarded. I had a responsibility to train men to be Marines and mold them so that they had the best possible baseline to take into battle and to bring them back alive. This was a crucial responsibility.

The philosophy of that experience remains the core of how I conduct myself. Being a notorious devil dog reinforced the idea that everyone is of value, and leaders should strive to bring out the best in people. Without it, you can't reach the other main goal of the drill instruction: building a strong team. It is incredibly difficult for 80 recruits to become a unit that can accomplish tasks as a single force, but it happens every 13 weeks.

Today, I take those lessons and apply them as part of organizational dynamics within my own company. I got very good at identifying shortcomings and helping individuals improve them, as well as teaching team members to rely on each other's strengths in order to counterbalance individual weaknesses.

Having trained two platoons of recruits, I earned a promotion to senior drill instructor with three junior drill instructors reporting to me. As a Sergeant, I was the youngest senior drill instructor on the depot and was in charge of one of the few all-Sergeant drill instructor teams created. This was not only an honor but something that was rare then and even today.

It was now my turn to control the drill instruction team and mold the recruits. As a senior drill instructor, I graduated eight platoons of Marines to serve in foreign climes and various places across the Corps. To date, several hundred stay in contact one way or another, though several have passed on. Most of them have been successful, and, for the most part, I like to think that I had some positive influence on their achievements.

Life-Changing Experience – The Impact to Your View of the World (1983)

Preparation

I was promoted to Staff Sergeant (meritoriously and ahead of my peers) on October 2, 1982, just two years after my prior promotion.

During that window, I got married again – this time to a woman whose father was former Navy. I was enamored with her from the day I met her. With my new wife I also gained a family, including two children from a prior marriage.

After a long day on the drill field, the world my wife and stepkids inhabited was my peaceful respite from the 18-hour days I spent with each platoon, but my work took a huge toll on our new family. Upon completion of my tour on the drill field, I moved them all to live with my wife's parents in Pennsylvania and then headed to my new assignment in North Carolina. Although we all knew what was coming, it was heart-wrenching to leave them behind.

Life Lesson:
Two is better than one, but both must realize what life in the military is really like.

I reported into Marine Aircraft Group 12, 3rd Marine Aircraft Wing, New River Air Station, New River, North Carolina, as a seasoned veteran of sorts, and was assigned as Acting Group Intelligence Chief. I was now a former Drill Instructor, a Scout Sniper, an Infantryman, and an Intelligence Chief by designation. Some people might have found that intimidating, but for me, I was simply embarking on my next challenge.

Lesson Learned:
You can make a mistake – just don't make the same mistake twice.

I hung out at the Group headquarters for a period, but the desk job didn't excite me. I knew that an Intelligence Chief position was coming available with a Squadron that was deploying under the 24th Marine Amphibious Unit (MAU), and I wanted to be there. I talked with several helicopter pilots assigned to the unit and got my name added to a list to be considered for the Intelligence Chief for Marine Medium Helicopter Squadron-162 (HMM-162).

For the first time, I had to prove I had the whole package of experience, background, education, and abilities in order to be considered for the position. Nothing about this position would be a given, and it turned into a valuable lesson I'd look back on many times.

The Battleground

With some effort, I was named the Intelligence Chief for HMM-162 (soon to be HMM-162 (Reinforced)) the same month I reported, December 1982. I was excited and was preparing myself to deploy to the Mediterranean. As the Squadron prepared for deployment, things were heating up in the Middle East and Lebanon was in trouble.

You see, in August 1982, troops from the United States, France, and Italy deployed to Beirut, Lebanon, on a peacekeeping mission. U.S. Marines comprised the American component of the multinational force. At the time, Lebanon was in the grips of a bloody civil war that had only worsened following Israel's 1982 invasion. The civil war was further escalated by external countries supporting various Lebanese factions and militia groups.

The 24th MAU deployed in May 1983 as part of a multinational peacekeeping force. The 24th MAU consisted of Battalion Landing Team 1/8 (1st Battalion, 8th Marine Regiment), Marine Medium Helicopter Squadron 162 (HMM-162 (Reinforced)), and Marine Amphibious Service Support Group 24. During this time, I had multiple tasks to support the mission of the Squadron, one of which was to set up reconnaissance locations to ensure we had early warning at our location at

Beirut International Airport (BIA).

I was also responsible for providing visual confirmation of militia elements that were surveying Marine locations at the airport. From my perch on one of the towers at the corner of said airport, I used binoculars to look through the windows of high-rise apartments that militia soldiers were using to take potshots at 1st Battalion, 8th Marine Regiment personnel along the front lines.

Throughout the months leading up to October 1983, these same positions would be used to call in multi-rocket launcher fire on our positions – specifically, our helicopter base. I fired three shots just prior to the multi-rocket launcher fire, one shot to get distance and wind, and two shots to illuminate the spotters. I was not permitted to return fire, only to mark my targets.

Reporters?

From the time we made our first landing at the BIA, I had been approached by multiple reporters. At each encounter, they were rude, self-important, unprofessional, and in many ways, not very good reporters. It felt like they were working against us (the Peacekeeping Force) at every turn. In general, I avoid reporters even to this day; however, I believe that I have matured (I'm more seasoned now) and can at least tolerate them.

> **Lesson Learned:**
> *Be leery of the Press – they generally have their own agenda, and it is not helpful to your situation.*

I did have one very positive encounter with a reporter from WMAQ, an NBC affiliate. My commanding officer had asked me to do an interview with some reporter from my home state, specifically, the Chicago area. I was less than happy, but orders are orders, so I participated in the multiple interview sessions.

Much to my surprise, [Paul Hogan](#) was just a consummate professional. He never set me up, he always told me exactly what he was going to ask and talk about, and he let me be me. Paul won an Emmy Award for the documentary and story titled, "Three Marines" – which was well deserved – and kept in contact over the years until his death in 1993.

Tragedy Strikes

Things continued to heat up in Beirut. Reality set in suddenly when one of the rockets I had been giving warnings about got far too close for comfort.

I was inside a makeshift bunker when one of many rockets from multi-rocket launchers fell on our position. The sound was deafening, like race cars going top speed on a paved track. The rumbling was pretty much all I could hear before the explosion from the rockets as they hit the ground. Having no control in a situation where you know you are in very real bodily danger is the worst kind of feeling – or so I thought.

During one of those attacks, our makeshift bunker collapsed. For a moment I was buried under dirt and the twisted metal remains of the bunker. I couldn't breathe, and when I tried, dirt threatened to fill my lungs. After what felt like hours or years, I was able to push my arm up. Another eon later, a Corpsman grabbed my arm and pulled me out from underneath as the rockets continued to fall around us.

I will be forever in debt to that Corpsman. I had already started making peace with my maker by the time he found me.

A couple of our Marines took some shrapnel, but all were able to recover very quickly. In those short moments, I saw unparalleled leadership and self-sacrifice from Marines and Sailors who were maybe in their late teens or early twenties.

> **Life Lesson:**
> *Leaders are forged from the most unexpected sources; you just need to look at the signs.*

It is incredible to watch real leadership in action.

Our sacrifice was not over, though. We continued to be attacked on a daily basis before a sudden and quiet lull set us all on edge. 0622 on Sunday morning, October 23, 1983, a suicide bomber driving a 19-ton truck penetrated the security perimeter of the building housing Marines and Sailors of Battalion Landing Team 1/8. The truck crashed into the lobby, and its payload detonated.

It was the largest non-nuclear explosion recorded at that time. 241 Service Members died, 220 of them Marines.

The heroics I saw from the helicopter crews who headed to the blast, making every effort to evacuate the wounded, were the stuff of legends. They were fishing Marines out of the rubble, Marines without limbs, their eyes and ears gone, and taking them to our aircrews who were waiting to get them to the ships and to medical personnel.

I was a crewman and aerial gunner then. You cannot unsee what I saw that day.

As I was manning my gun, covering the crew chief and the wounded who were being piled into the helicopter, all I could hear was intense screaming bouncing off the metal hull. I reached out for the hand of a wounded Marine. Instead, I realized I was holding on to an arm that was completely severed.

These are the sorts of tragedies of war that no one wants to talk about. You have to compartmentalize the overwhelming scenes and emotional experiences so that you can somehow live with them the rest of your life. For me, like so many servicemen and women before and after, this has been one of the most difficult challenges in my life.

To this day, I firmly believe there was a reason for all of that. The experience allowed me to understand and treasure human life as a precious commodity that should be protected.

The Grasshopper

I reported to a 1st Lieutenant named Michael F. King, who was a helicopter pilot as well as designated an S-2 Officer (Intelligence Officer). He was one of the finest men I have ever known.

When people have written about Michael, they talk about him being a Foreign Service brat and a rink knocker (a reference to his Naval Academy background), but he was much more than that. He provided me with insight earned through his travels that helped me understand different cultures that I had not yet been exposed to.

He was a leader and could rally men to get results. He made *me* a better leader. Sometimes leaders are just born to be leaders. I will forever miss his counsel: Captain King was killed in a helicopter crash on October 31, 1988.

In 1983, though, he was still with us and was the kind of man who gave everyone who knew him the strength to pick up and carry on despite so much tragedy all at once. This and so many other times, he showed us that you can take those experiences in life, both grotesque and beautiful, and embrace them or you can allow them to consume you. I chose to cling to the good and find ways to use those scars to help others.

It was a life-changing set of events by anyone's standards, but it helped prepare me for future conflicts along the way. That week, there were a lot of heroes who did extraordinary things, and a lot of Marines burst from their youths to take charge and lead.

Just two days after the bombing of Battalion Landing Team 1/8, the United States invaded Grenada under Operation Urgent Fury. It was October 25, 1983. The unit scheduled to relieve us, 22nd Marine Amphibious Unit, was diverted to participate in the operation. We were all concerned that we would need to stay in Beirut for an extended period, but U.S. forces completed the mission in four days. We were overjoyed to hear that our relief unit was on its way to Lebanon.

Members of the strike force that came in from Grenada to relieve my unit received 5,000 medals for merit and valor and then set off for the next big hotspot without hesitation. They demonstrated handily how leadership and honor move hand in hand with integrity and valor.

The Fallout

In the days after the suicide bombing, responding to inquiries from families who were trying to find their missing or injured loved ones was incredibly difficult. Unfortunately, my family had to experience this terrifying uncertainty as well. I knew where I was, but apparently no one else did.

I was listed as missing in action for a total of four days. Finally, I was able to get a ship-to-shore message to my brother (a fellow Marine at New River Air Station) reassuring him that I was still alive. It's easy to forget that the pain of war is felt at home just as much as in the war zone, especially when an entire city like Camp Lejeune is in shock, waiting for any news about the welfare of friends and family.

My last mission in Lebanon, on November 28, 1983, was as part of a reconnaissance team to the Bekaa Valley. We could hear the hundreds of rounds being fired from the USS New Jersey toward Druze and Shi'ite positions in the hills overlooking Beirut as they rumbled over our heads. Thirty or more of these massive projectiles, each the size of a flying Volkswagen bus, rained down on a Syrian command post in the area, killing the general who was commanding the Syrian forces in Lebanon and several other senior officers.

Although I was finally heading back to the United States, much to my relief, it was bittersweet. I received divorce papers, and my second marriage unfortunately ended. After a mandatory waiting period, the paperwork was finalized in April 1984.

TWA Hijacking – The Algiers Operation (1985)

I returned from my last deployment just in time for Christmas. Of course, by that time I was single again, so I headed home to Chicago for a well-deserved vacation with my family. I continued to be followed by the press, with multiple reporters trying to interview my brother and me during our leave.

I shunned most of them, but I did one interview with the Lake Zurich Herald. Most military folks don't really talk about their experiences in war – or otherwise. I certainly wasn't interested in discussing much with the press after my experiences in Lebanon.

During my time back in the States, I had the good fortune of reconnecting with a woman I had known since junior high school. We were married shortly thereafter in June 1984. It turned out to be a really good decision, but it wasn't long before I was deployed back to the Mediterranean.

We were expecting to be sent back to Beirut, but life had its own plans. As we were heading across the Atlantic on June 14, 1985, a TWA passenger jet (TWA Flight 847) was hijacked in Athens, Greece. It was diverted to Beirut International Airport with 152 passengers on board.

The hijackers initially released 19 passengers in return for fuel, then took off for Algiers while threatening the lives of the remaining hostages. The powers that be considered storming the aircraft but ultimately did not give that order. Since our task force was already en route to the Mediterranean, we were diverted to the coast of Algiers.

We participated in the planning of special operations around the event, and several members of our task force were also flown into Algiers itself to assess and be briefed on the

> **Philosophical Statement Number Six:**
> *Leaders must check their emotions at the door – decisions must be made based on facts, and knee-jerk reactions never end well.*

situation.

At the same time in Algiers, the hijackers released another 20 passengers, refueled, then headed back to Beirut. They sent us a message after landing again, brutally beating and then shooting U.S. Navy Diver Robert Dean Stethem in the head. His body was dumped on the runway.

A dozen new hijackers got on the plane in Beirut, then the group headed back to Algiers. Our task force continued monitoring the situation off the coast as decisions were made regarding if or when Special Operators would storm the plane. The hijackers flew to Beirut a third time with 40 Americans who were subsequently dispersed throughout the city to block any rescue attempts.

As we concluded our Mediterranean deployment and headed back to the United States, I reviewed all the decisions that were made as part of an after-action report. I believe that had the leaders who were making the decisions reacted with emotion, those hostages would have died in a raid with no positive results.

The whole event is a great example of leadership in action. After all, leaders must check their emotions at the door. The hardest decisions have to be made based on facts – knee-jerk reactions never end well.

From 1976 to 1985, I was given incredible opportunities to learn leadership skills and refine them through formal and hands-on training. There are few organizations that allow people so young to develop these skills at such a fast pace and with so little room to make mistakes as the military. I'm thankful every day that my grandfather suggested and supported my enlistment.

I use almost all of these concepts from those early years to various degrees in my current position. Basic leadership skills are essential to success – they give you a solid foundation upon which to develop more complex methodologies for shaping and guiding the people around you.

Chapter 2: Supporting the National Defense

Panama – Learning Strategic Importance (1985-1989)

The Core of Leadership

Although the time spent in the Mediterranean was exciting and gave me many opportunities for seeing the positive results of good leadership, I left the Air Wing and returned to the infantry in 1985. My wife and I built our first home in Sneads Ferry, North Carolina, and settled there with our oldest daughter and a second child on the way due in October.

I was stationed at nearby Camp Lejeune, where I joined the 2nd Marine Division, reporting to the G-2 (the Intelligence department) the same month my second daughter was due. There, I was given an assignment as Special Security Office (SSO) Chief, whose duty was to manage the highly sensitive documents and other information for the entire 2nd Marine Division. Needless to say, the sheer amount of data involved was monumental. Another aspect of the job was working very closely with the division's signals intelligence unit, which was housed in the same building.

Lesson Learned:
The ability to put information in compartments and have it at your fingertips when needed is useful, but understanding its value is essential.

Compartmentalizing information became crucial to success here, since there was simply so much coming in and going out – one poorly organized communication could be catastrophic. The data we worked with contained multiple levels of Top Secret and

Special Compartmented Information (SCI), as well as other sensitive data; sorting and labeling each one correctly meant that data that was "for your eyes only" remained that way.

After so much time, working with this kind of information in this way created something akin to a reflex that I continue to use daily. The skill turned out to be invaluable when dealing with corporate politics.

As part of this job, I had my first taste of briefing senior military officials, including senior political leaders, on various national defense topics. Having access to all the additional information gave me a bigger-picture view of the geopolitical situation in any given scenario. I could easily pluck out the information that was vital to both my own leadership and the Commanding General so that the best decisions were made for the 2nd Marine Division.

Lesson Learned: Indecision is a decision regardless of the situation.

Although most of the decisions we supplied intel for were life-and-death matters with little room for error, being part of that team was an excellent learning experience in how individual areas should interact and how to anticipate the critical dependencies for each function based on the current context. It was different from how civilian corporations would function but nonetheless important for a greater understanding of organizational operations.

I served under a leader who continues to influence my own views on leadership day-to-day. General Alfred Gray (29th Commandant of the Marine Corps from July 1, 1987, until his retirement on June 30, 1991) was a Marine's Marine. He enlisted in the Marine

> **Philosophical Beliefs (apply to both military and civilian worlds):**
> He (General Alfred Gray) summarized the core of leadership – civilian or military: "If you come and join my Marines, I want you to know that your number one job is to take care of the men and women you are privileged to lead."

Corps as a Private and rose all the way to the top of the rank structure, rather than entering as an officer.

By definition, serving in the enlisted ranks made Gray a "mustang," which generally commands more respect in the Corps because of the combination of officer smarts and enlisted practicality. He had a mantra that has stuck with me and applies to both military and civilian worlds: "If you come and join my Marines, I want you to know that **your number one job is to take care of the men and women you are privileged to lead.**" This was how he summarized the core of leadership – civilian or military.

The Canal

Shortly after being honored with a promotion to Gunnery Sergeant in August 1987, a call came in from Headquarters Marine Corps to check my willingness to deploy again so soon after my last deployment. Of course, my answer was, "I serve at the pleasure of the Commandant," only half-jokingly.

After a bit of a laugh on the other end of the phone, I was asked to call them back on a

secure line. Since I had already been seeing information on planning activities for Central America and, more specifically, background intelligence on the scene in Panama, I put the pieces together quickly when I got the call from HQ.

They asked me if I would accept an assignment as the G-2 Intelligence Operations Chief for 6th Marine Expeditionary Force (MEF), with the understanding that I may be deploying to Central America. I reported to 6th MEF in October 1987.

Most civilians don't really understand what a military family goes through during a crisis that may require intervention. The public sees a headline in the news or television reporting, but for those of us who must execute a military mission, the situation is extremely difficult and very real.

An inherent part of leadership is the ability to have compassion and empathy among the many voices that are whispering in your ear while you are making a hard decision. It's not about emotions; it is about managing the emotions. Checking emotions at the door does not mean you leave the empathy behind, however.

Although I was still in North Carolina, learning that my wife was pregnant with our third child in March 1988 made my heart drop into my stomach. What she didn't know was that I was being briefed for an operation in Panama at the same time. I was activated on April 2 and reported to the Command Element, 5th MEB for transportation to the Republic of Panama with advanced force operations under "Operation Just Cause." They officially reassigned me to contingency operations at this time, too.

There were no indications in the press or otherwise that the U.S. was preparing to invade Panama, so when I went home that day to pack my equipment and the few additional items I was authorized to bring, it was under a crushing weight. I wasn't allowed to tell my wife where I was going or what I was doing, even as she flashed worried glances at me.

It was the hardest thing for both of us. For me, leaving my pregnant wife and two small children at home was beyond upsetting, and I imagine she was a lot more freaked out than she ever let on.

The Command Element were the first combat troops to arrive in Panama. We were tasked with advanced force operations in support of the planned invasion that would eventually occur on December 20 of the same year. I led Marines in the intelligence operations organization at that time, and many of my charges were getting their first real taste of combat.

There weren't many reporters on the ground in Panama (remember, we didn't give a lot of clues that there was an invasion coming), so naturally the events were underreported. But after an attack on the Marines guarding the Arraijan fuel tank farm near Howard Air Force Base in mid-April 1988, we started to get a little press.

The reports trickling into the news, unfortunately, stated that we were firing at ghosts, but the reality was that we were just one of many locations attacked in a coordinated effort by the Panamanian Defense Forces. One Marine was killed during one of the many incidents at the petroleum tank farm. But, of course, the story doesn't end there. The Panamanians also came after us at the Marine Barracks, where our intelligence feeds and command post were located.

I can attest that the ghosts were very real, as the 60mm mortar rounds and automatic 7.62 bullets were felt by many of my Marines. They were also felt at home, as the Marine families left behind were finally getting some word on our whereabouts.

To the Military Command's credit, no family was left wondering what was going on with their loved ones. Instead, they immediately were given updates reassuring them that everyone was accounted for. It took about 45 days in country, but I was finally allowed to call my wife to help calm her and my children's fears. It was still about eight months before the planned invasion date.

Lesson Learned:
Never believe what the Press reports; their reports are generally wrong and certainly biased, and the best-case scenario is that the reports have small pieces of the truth.

Life Lesson:
As a Leader, you must deal in facts and take a fact-based approach to all situations, especially the decision-making process.

Innovation Pays Off

Despite some of the terrifying things that happened early in my time in Panama, my team also had the opportunity to test new intelligence technology that would make it easier for us to ensure that the best possible actionable intelligence went to the war fighters on the ground.

In a time before cell phones and GPS were really in a usable form, the satellite imagery we were using was amazing. Using this new technology, satellite information traveling from Washington could get to the ground forces in minutes rather than hours. We could literally see actual images of the fighting and the attacks occurring outside our own front gate more or less at the same time that our Virginia counterparts did.

It was a game changer.

Even though we were breaking a lot of new ground in Panama, I couldn't help but worry about my family back home. So when relief forces arrived after about 90 days in country, it was a cause for celebration. They would take over our operations and put the wheels of Operation Just Cause fully in motion, take over Panama and establish civilian rule.

I rejoined my stateside unit just in time for the birth of my third daughter in late 1988. In November, I had been due for orders to a special kind of Marines position known as a "B-Billet." The B-Billet Designator includes positions like Drill Instructor, Recruiter, and Training Instructor, but for me, it was a joint assignment with Naval Space Command in Dahlgren, Virginia.

It wasn't a random assignment; in fact, it was due to my work with satellites and other space technology that provided intel to the war fighters that I was even considered. But when it was offered to me, I accepted it eagerly and began the process of moving my family to our new station in Virginia.

Life Lesson:
As best you can, keep work at work. When you can spend time with the family, be there with the family – really be there.

Decision-Making – The Impact on Lives (1990-1992)

Supporting National Decision-Making

I was the only enlisted Marine on the naval base when I reported to Naval Space Command in January 1989. I was ahead of my family to get some of the more mundane things out of the way, like arranging housing and getting the lay of the land. Getting acclimated to my duties there was challenging, but the rewards were immense. As the Space Operations Center (SPOC) Intelligence Chief, I was totally overwhelmed by the magnitude of strategic importance but thrilled for the experience.

My job duties were wide-ranging. I briefed senior military staff from the Department of Defense, the State Department, and the White House, as well as various Heads of State. But, because things were heating up in the Middle East, a number of assets were also being redirected to support Central Command. This created additional tasks for my team and me, including working with our counterparts in the United States Space Command, integrating space intelligence and naval intelligence, and continuing the work on the same technology we used to get actionable intelligence to fighters in Panama.

I was additionally assigned to the China and the Rest of the World (CROW) Space Panel of the Weapons and Space Systems Intelligence Committee as the Command Representative. I was able to glean a great deal of insight into the U.S. strategy for our space assets as a whole from this experience, making the rest of my duty much easier since, once again, I had the appropriate context to present during briefs.

Space Operations presented many opportunities to observe and practice elements of different leadership techniques that were being modeled around me. It was a really great time in my career, and I learned a great deal about the kind of information most needed to make major high-level decisions. Two Marine Officers in particular stick with me due to their leadership styles. I still have a huge amount of respect for both of them and appreciate having had the opportunity to learn from their examples.

Colonel Chuck Geiger (Commander Naval Space Command: Apr 1990 – May 1990) was direct and to the point but always listened and asked questions that were designed to make his charges think. He was undeniably a leader of men. Lieutenant Colonel Steve Sonnenberg was (and is) a gentleman's gentleman. He was a brainiac but also made the effort to meet people at their own level without being condescending. There's an art to this, there's no doubt. He taught me that people matter.

No Room for Indecision

In January 1991, I was temporarily assigned to the U.S. Central Command Headquarters in Tampa, Florida, for duty in intelligence collections. There were lots of opportunities to expand on my experiences in space operations and strategic intelligence here as I supported General Schwarzkopf's team and the war fighters on the ground in the Middle

East with real-time actionable intelligence from our space assets.

By the 17th, Operation "Desert Storm" was officially launched and I was charged with using U.S. Navy meteorological assets to detect Iraqi SCUD missile launches targeted at Coalition Forces on the move. As the offensive was just beginning, I got a call from General Schwarzkopf himself! I was floored, but as the senior person in the command center at the time, it was my job to take calls like that. He wanted confirmation of an Iraqi launch site, which I provided. He ended the call with two words I'll never forget, "Thanks, Gunny."

It was my only interaction with one of the greatest Generals in U.S. history, but I'll never forget it. I like to believe that my team contributed in a small way to minimize the casualties for the Coalition Forces throughout Operation Desert Storm. Every experience in that capacity, including the impact of the decision-making processes of Central Command, profoundly impacted the way I made decisions as a member of leadership. It was where I really internalized the idea that there was no place for indecision as a leader.

I picked up my duties as SPOC Intelligence Chief at the Naval Space Command upon completion of the Desert Storm campaign. This job took me to U.S. Space Command at Peterson Air Base on a regular basis to conduct interactive meetings, as well as provide updates and insight into my mission with U.S. Central Command. Working in this strategic planning environment taught me a great deal about managing space assets, and I received significant informal education on the related technological advancements of the prior decade. My expertise allowed

> **Lesson Learned:**
> *Always study your leaders and glean the best traits and qualities from them.*

me to identify specific items that should be pushed forward to the Commanders on the ground, though I spent a lot of time sorting intelligence for intelligence's sake from the actionable information war fighters could use on the battlefield.

Enhancing My Education

With Desert Storm and the invaluable experience gained from it in the rear-view mirror, it was back to the classroom for some theory to add to my practical experience. It was a big year, really. I was asked to join the ranks of the Navy Chiefs by the Command Master Chief.

It was an incredible honor to be asked, but it was a lot more complicated on my end than a simple yes or no. Even though Chief Petty Officer in the Navy was a premier enlisted rank and the leadership backbone of the Navy, I was still a Marine. That meant I had to get a lot of special permission before I could accept the title. Needless to say, this was not a common honor for a Marine.

But, before becoming a Chief, I had to undergo Chiefs' initiation. It involves difficult teamwork challenges that are often unpleasant. The experience humbled me and served well to demonstrate just how much more important teamwork is in those kinds of tasks, far beyond the accomplishments of any individual. Leadership, I learned during initiation, was a true calling.

At the end of the initiation ceremony, they officially pin the Chief Petty Officer's rank on the recipient's uniform. But, again, because I was a Marine and not in the Navy, I had to get special permission from the Commandant of the Marine Corps to even wear the insignia, and even then it was only allowed for 24 hours.

This probably sounds like a lot of pageantry and pomp and circumstance for what was essentially an honorary title, but it was a very unique situation and a big deal.

Not all my education was in the field that year, though. We continued to live in Dahlgren, Virginia, and I commuted daily to participate in the Senior Enlisted Intelligence Program at the then-named Defense Intelligence College in Washington, D.C. My concentration there was in Far East Studies and Collection Management in an academic environment that was much different than any required by my previous assignments.

The pressure was very low, aside from making dissertation deadlines. It was a long, blissful year to focus on study and debate on a wide spectrum of leadership and management topics as they related to military intelligence operations.

Lesson Learned:
Knowledge is power.

While I was attending this program, I took the opportunity to earn an Associate of Science in General Studies and graduated both programs in June 1992. But with every major jump ahead, relocation seemed to follow. This time, I was headed to Japan and my family moved to Illinois to be close to the grandparents. We would be separated for a year while I was on assignment overseas.

49

The Calm of Kyoto (1992-1993)

Meeting New Colleagues

The operational tempo was very high at my new command in Marine Aircraft Group 12, Marine Corps Air Station, Iwakuni, Japan, about 26 miles south of Hiroshima and 250 miles southwest of Kyoto. I was the Group Intelligence Chief of the fixed winged aircraft group. "Fixed winged" is one of many terms used to differentiate types of aircraft groups – essentially, we had lots of planes but no helicopters.

Support planning was my primary interest, and as I settled into my post and new responsibilities, I started working through a review of all contingency plans in place, as well as the intelligence support requirements for each. Since our primary missions in the area were the defense of Japan from North Korea and providing support to the Naval Fleet in the Pacific, my first steps were to get to know my regional Japanese counterparts and the capabilities of their Japanese Defense Forces (JDF).

My recent studies in the culture of the Far East and my early tour of duty in Okinawa helped me navigate in Japan and improved my communications with various colleagues in the JDF, as well as the Japanese Ministry of Defense, since I could partially speak the language. Because I needed to regularly meet with intelligence resources and assets in the region, I was able to travel extensively within Japan and to South Korea and Okinawa. Being part of an aircraft group made these many trips virtually painless, catching a 'hop' (space available) on cargo planes going back and forth to multiple destinations.

Meeting and Greeting

Since travel was easy, attending official (and unofficial) events and meeting with Japanese officials were both regular elements of my job. These were both useful for networking with others in Japan and for really becoming part of the local Marine culture.

Marines on Iwakuni participate in a fun run (there is nothing fun about this run). The Annual Mount Fuji Climbing Race is an exercise in, well, extreme exercise, where Marines run up Mount Fuji. The 21-kilometer race covers everything from paved roads to wooded trails, steep rocky slopes, and jagged vertical stairs. It was by far one of the toughest runs I completed (in July 1992).

But, of course, it was more than a "fun" run. I met several participants from Kyoto. I was very interested in the Imperial Capital after studying Far East cultures the previous year, but I wouldn't get there until after contingency-planning exercises in South Korea in late August. Between the run up Mt. Fuji and my trip to Kyoto, I was able to do some sightseeing, including the wooden Kintai Bridge, Iwakuni Castle, and Kikkō Park, where there are samurai-era residences. The Samurai influence was infused in the city's culture.

Let me back up a little bit – after all, August 1992 was a busy month. Earlier that month, I was in Tokyo for briefings and one very fortuitous cocktail function. Japanese industry leaders were mingling with U.S. officials that night, of course, but so was a particular nurse I had known in Okinawa (the lovely lady who stole my heart and whose parents refused to consider an engagement).

Life Lesson:
Try never to burn bridges with people even if there is some pain involved, because you never know when you will meet them again.

It was like a scene in a movie, bumping into her that night. I had no idea she'd be at the function, but as I moved around the room, there she was. It was a surprise to say the least. We exchanged pleasantries, and during our conversation she introduced me to her husband, who was a high-ranking executive.

We chatted about their family, where they lived, and all those kinds of topics people who had once been close can easily spend hours catching up on. Before they left, she and her husband invited me to their family home in Kyoto, and I eagerly accepted.

It was probably best that we didn't get married because 15 years later she was in a much better place than I could have provided. We still had those memories to rebuild a friendship upon, though, and for that I was thankful.

I went to Kyoto as planned and was able to

have dinner with them. Their hilltop home was amazing, with a view of the Nijo castle (built in 1679) and all the quiet solitude of the countryside. I still have contacts with both her and her husband to this day and continue to interact with him on a business level.

To Understand Japan….

Life Lesson:
Take time to disconnect from your daily tasks and routine, make time to reenergize and refocus on things that drive your personal needs, and learn to take this time as you need it.

To understand Japan, you must understand the history of the Japanese people. I returned to Kyoto several times while stationed at Iwakuni, simply to soak in the culture built upon those rich traditions. I was lucky enough to be in Kyoto in November 1992 for Culture Day, a Japanese holiday.

Local people were dressed in traditional clothes from the Edo period, and traditional Japanese food was served at events around the city. I learned a lot from the students I met at different locations around Kyoto that day. They taught me much more about the culture of Japan than I had learned in school.

While I was in Japan, I learned to assess people in a different way, to make every effort to understand their perspectives, and to understand how their culture impacts their decision-making processes.

I honestly believe that this is key to the ability to read people as well. Relationship building can't be productive without several ingredients, and meeting people where they live is one of the most vital.

Closing the Chapter – Retirement (1993-1996)

The Next Duty Station

Leaving Japan in April 1993 was a mixed experience. I got to return home to my family, which I absolutely wanted to do, but I also had to leave a lot of stones unturned since I didn't have unlimited time to explore the country. That's life; it's full of all sorts of trade-offs.

My family and I moved to California to report for my new post as Intelligence Operations Chief for 1st Marine Division G-2. This was my fourth tour of duty with an Infantry Unit, but I was looking forward to some time at Division Headquarters and a much less aggressive deployment schedule than I'd become accustomed to.

My team of approximately 30 Marines helped gather raw intelligence and provide actionable information to the Commanding General and his staff. Since I'd already worked with other high-level staff, I knew what was expected and even above and beyond as we were asked to address various strategic hotspots like the Korean Peninsula, the Balkans, Somalia, and parts of Southwest Asia.

The experience we had collected as a team proved to be exactly what the senior leadership needed. In fact, they came to rely upon me as a trusted advisor, which was crucial to my own success and the success of my team. I never wanted the spotlight, so working behind the scenes to inform and influence high-level geopolitical and military situational decisions was ideal for me. Not only did I get to mature my leadership and

Lesson Learned:
From a personal perspective, you must decide how you should operate based on your own personality traits. Know yourself.

management skills with my team, but I also was learning how to cultivate trust-based relationships with the leadership levels above me. Managing up will be discussed in a future chapter.

Being invisible, but indispensable, turned out to be the key to a major promotion in January 1994 to Master Sergeant (E-8). It was a great way to kick off the year!

Deploying Tech to the Field

When it comes to the Marine Corps Enlisted Ranks, there wasn't a lot higher to climb. At this point, I was very close to the top of the enlisted ladder, with only E-9s, Master Gunnery Sergeants, Sergeant Majors, and the Sergeant Major of the Marine Corps (the senior ranking enlisted Marine, who is hand-selected by the Commandant) above me. My team continued to support operations in the Pacific Theater and in Europe when required, and it was generally business as usual with a shiny new title.

Life ebbs and flows, though, and so do opportunities. A colleague had recently decided to retire, making the position of Regimental Intelligence Chief available. This wasn't the Intelligence Chief of just ANY regiment, it was for the most decorated regiment in the Marine Corps: the 5th Marine Regiment. The history of this group alone was reason enough to want to be a part of it, and its reputation was like a cherry on top. Since the regiment was getting a new Commanding Officer as well, it put me in the perfect position to take the vacant Intelligence Chief position.

With an excellent recommendation and help from the Division G-2 Officer and my contacts at Headquarters Marine Corps, I was honored with the much-coveted position in the 5th MR.

From the moment I reported in July 1994, I was supporting the Battalions of 5th Marines with intelligence, leveraging my previous relationships at the Division Headquarters and with various colleagues at the national level.

My team was busy developing the ability to bring direct analytics to the war fighting units deployed on the ground. Our testing began with several mechanized infantry operations at 29 Palms training area, where we tested our ability to operate analytical computer systems in the desert environment.

We were successfully able to connect satellite communications to computer systems in trucks in the field. Although we didn't get the opportunity to test these systems in real combat conditions, the simulations were effective enough to prove the concept would be useful in the field. Remember, the compact cell phone had not yet been developed.

I worked with our reconnaissance teams to increase the effectiveness of reporting from their covert positions to the regimental headquarters. We were still using radio multichannel with encryption to transmit data to the teams behind the lines for analysis. The ability to leverage wireless communications was not yet available.

Reflecting on 20 Years of Service

Although I had exceeded my own expectations in the Marines, I had been worried that I wasn't going to be able to be competitive in the civilian world with only an associate's degree. My new self-imposed mission was to finish a bachelor's degree by the time I was eligible to retire so that I would have more options should I choose to leave the military.

I also made a mental note to avoid casinos at all costs.

Since my military experience had taught me to look three years out and assess where I wanted to be and how that would affect my family, it was important that I have a plan in place. That was the impetus behind going back to school and the mechanism that helped me stay focused until graduation in December 1995, with a BS in Liberal Arts.

I learned so much from being in the Marines and will forever be in debt to my grandfather for his nudging me gently in that direction, but after so many years, I knew it would be better for my family to set down roots somewhere for good. I wasn't sure how I'd navigate the corporate world after being part of such a strict and disciplined environment for so long or where we'd settle, but it was definitely time to look outside the Marines.

My wife helped me work through the many options we had available for establishing a permanent home. We both wrote down pros and cons of each location we were considering on large pieces of paper hung on the refrigerator with magnets. It took several months before the fridge lists came down.

Life Lesson:
Always be willing to make the tough decisions, that is best for you and your family, and make sure a job is fun – when it stops being fun, it ceases to be a job and becomes a burden.

We started planning for a civilian life in October 1995, which made the November 10 Marine Corps Birthday celebration a bittersweet one. Unlike other military branches, Marines gather to celebrate the past, present, and future of the service, no matter where they may be in the world. This would be my last Marine Ball as an active-duty Marine. Sometimes, protocol and celebration are important.

Reflecting at the table of the fallen Marine, I pondered over all the service people who were lost over the years, and those that I knew and had counted among my most valuable friends and mentors. Although we didn't make it official until the end of 1995, I knew deep down that I would be retiring after 20 years and 27 days of active service.

My wife and I had also found the place where we'd start our lives as a civilian family: San Antonio, Texas. It was exciting and terrifying at the same time because there were so many unknowns. We spent the summer of 1996 finishing up the preparations to start over, my retirement closing in at an astonishing pace.

But the Marines don't let their own go without a little celebration. The Commanding Officer of the 5th Marine Regiment hosted a military retirement formation for me. I was allowed to command the regiment by dismissing the troops, an honor I will never forget. This was my last official act as a Master Sergeant in the United States Marine Corps. I officially retired from active service on October 30, 1996.

THE TITLE
It cannot be inherited,
Nor can it ever be purchased.
You, nor anyone else alive
Can buy it for any price.
It is impossible to rent,
And it cannot be lent.
You alone and our own
Have earned it
With your sweat, blood and lives.
You own it forever.
The Title,
UNITED STATES MARINE

Chapter 3: Starting Over – Reality of the Civilian World

Defense Industrial Complex – Teaching

My wife and I had made our decision to relocate to San Antonio, Texas, based on the great experiences I had there while on different temporary duty assignments. With the car packed up, we followed after the movers and all of our possessions. The first day of the trip to San Antonio from California was an endurance test. The kids alternated between crying and bemoaning the changes that they were forced into making in schools, friends, and other vital facets of life at that age.

It wasn't an easy decision for any of us, but the idea of remaining in California with the tax system there and the growing disconnect between the military and the local population was just not going to be sustainable. At least Texas, and specifically San Antonio, was a welcoming city. And as I would find out, jobs in the Defense industry were plentiful. The support system for veterans was impressive, with multiple bases located around the city plus a major military hospital and a regional VA hospital that offered a range of services – all things we were accustomed to on a military base.

We took a huge chance moving across the country with no job and no home to move into. We had 90 days of military pay before my retirement pay would kick in, and it proved to be all I needed. We rented a home for a year and began the search for a good area to build a house in that would be well within our budget. We didn't want anything too fancy, just a modest home large enough for the kids to grow, and a place we could all make friends and put down roots.

At the same time, it felt like I was being interviewed daily, as I searched for a job that was a good fit. I leveraged all of my contacts, the military placement service, and Department of Defense job boards to try to find a good-paying job. What I learned very quickly was that I was going to have to start over at the bottom and work back up.

It was somewhat demoralizing to be not-so-subtly told that 20 years of work experience really didn't count for much in the civilian workforce. I was also shocked to discover that many companies used military retirement benefits against an applicant by including that monthly pay as income in a twisted attempt to justify offering a lower salary than they would offer to civilian peers.

> **Lesson Learned:**
> Do not allow an employer to use a secondary source of income to justify a lower salary for a current position – it is just not right.

I got my lucky break, though, when I interviewed with the company that would become Lucent Technologies. A colleague from the Marines who I knew well just happened to be conducting the interview. A couple of hours later, I was offered a job as an instructor for the Unix operating system and an information-security application associated with the Air Forces security system. This was a great opportunity to begin to prove myself and start back on the road to success.

I had less experience (in civilian terms) than peers of the same age with the same education, but I needed to build my resume. It was a chance to make the difficult transition from the military to the civilian world, and moving into the civilian side of the Defense Industrial Complex was a good way to ease into a new environment and culture.

During the seven months I spent in that position, I worked with Bell Labs, attained several industry certifications, and co-wrote two manuals related to the information I was teaching. I taught several classes and numerous students over the course of a year. It was a very tedious time, but I was focused on catching up to and surpassing my peers. I was driven to succeed in this foreign space, so I also developed a career plan and timeline filled with goals and objectives to keep me on track. The extra planning, I reasoned, would help me catch up on the level of experience expected in my field.

Lesson Learned: Planning is essential in everything you do, and especially when your own career is at stake. Do not short-change yourself.

Since I was already significantly behind my peers, I decided that I could not spend a lot of time following the corporate promotion systems. Part of my plan was to move from one company to another where I could gain a step up in position, as well as in salary. Most hiring managers at that level look at whether you were a job hopper, a sure sign you won't be dependable as a member of the company, so it was a risky move.

In several interviews that I participated in for various Information Technology (IT) and Information Security (IS) jobs, I experienced pushback from the people I met with, as they expressed concerns about my short tenure in my current position. However, I found that when I explained why I was changing jobs (to be competitive with my peers), the rest of the interview process was much better. Honesty is the best policy, as they say.

Because I held a Top Secret/Sensitive Compartmented Information (TS/SCI) security clearance (which was a very high level), companies in San Antonio were often willing to overlook other potential risks, like the appearance of job-hopping. They needed people who had this clearance and could start work immediately.

I successfully made it through two different hiring processes while looking for a place to land after Lucent. Now I had to choose which job would be next and what its potential was to meet my personal goals and objectives.

Of the two job offers I had, one really caught my eye. It was interesting, promised to be exciting, and had the potential to provide some upward mobility. I would also have the chance to learn some new technologies and new use cases that might be applied to the wider commercial market. With that in mind, I resigned from Lucent Technologies and took a job at CACI International in the Automated Sciences Group as a Senior System Engineer.

Directed Energy Lab

Diversified Personalities

In the job I accepted, I was a defense contractor working at the Directed Energy Facility (a research laboratory now called the Tri-Service Research Laboratory-TSRL), running the Unix systems that supported the company's internal operations.

It was a deeply academic environment that included anechoic chambers and laboratory spaces for laser research, imaging, radiation, biology, microbiology, biochemistry, biomolecular research, tissue cultures, and proteomics. This was my first interaction with PhD-level scientists and other academics in a research environment.

Even though my primary function was ensuring that the Unix systems backup and recovery processes supporting the scientists were stable and that collected data was never lost, I still managed to get a pretty healthy education in the sciences. The background helped me better understand each group's needs. This background added to my knowledge from space systems and the multiple backup system strategy we used there to protect all the systems at the Directed Energy Lab from failing at the same time.

Any time I thought I was the smartest person in the room, I was quickly humbled simply by having conversations with some of the great minds in that facility. These were all people of great intellect, but they were generally not 'people' people. Getting to know them was challenging, but as I worked through various conversations, there was always some kind of common ground, even if I did sometimes have to study a topic or an issue so that I could adequately engage without getting out of my depth.

I also found myself learning conflict resolution hands on, as the unofficial referee in many heated conversations and debates between colleagues. It was generally pretty entertaining, even if I was used as a target for academic humor most of the time. You had to have some thick skin in that kind of environment! It would prove useful in future encounters with various people as I learned to navigate personalities quickly and adjust my perceptions on the fly.

In this organization, it was my job to help the scientists succeed with their research. Anything I could do to speed up their analysis or provide the database structure that would support their search criteria from a systems perspective was important to that end goal.

Proving a Negative

I functioned both as a system administrator with management responsibility and as the security administrator responsible for ensuring the protection of various algorithms, code, and other data. My most important task in almost every case was safeguarding information until a patent was approved and then helping secure that patent. Once I fully understood the scope of my role, it was simple to implement security controls that were primarily focused on protecting patent information.

Lesson Learned: Take the time to understand your customers' needs and desires, not just requirements but what is important (or even critical) to them.

If there was a need for more data storage or more memory, I would generally help provide the security-impact statements that could facilitate approvals, which at the time were viewed as a value-add capability.

Because of the nature of the work being done at this facility at that time, there was always the possibility of protests against some experiment or test being conducted, so we always had to consider how to safeguard data and recover it at a different location if the protests got violent. Contingency planning became a high priority and made it more difficult to justify redundant systems.

Bean counters generally don't see a need to spend research dollars on redundant systems, of course, unless their work is affected by a system outage and their data is lost. Imagine the outcry that would come from the finance people if their financial data wasn't available for them to analyze or they had reports that couldn't be delivered!

Lesson Learned:
Sometimes it is necessary to prove the negative.

Sometimes it felt like it might become necessary to prove a negative in order to secure even obviously needed computer and network equipment. What I mean by that is that it could have theoretically taken a simulated outage to prove that a real one would have very serious repercussions for both research and data.

I am not at all recommending this course of action in this day and age, but when an information system is not available, and more importantly when someone feels like they have lost their life's work, it's a memorable experience (for them) that can have major budgetary impacts.

The key to a positive outcome in a hypothetical like this is to ensure that the data and information are recoverable. Everyone understands the value of redundancy after a scare like that – you've proved a negative. If hypotheticals never happen, it can be hard for people to see just how impactful these situations can be without the proper precautions in place.

Data Protection – The Early Experience

The unclassified version of the mission of the Directed Energy Lab was essentially to conduct studies of emerging directed-energy weapons (including non-lethal weapons) and their effects on humans. Since a lot of what we did there was classified, the research itself was highly sensitive and required multiple physical and logical security controls.

Previous experiences in both offensive and defensive cybersecurity were extremely useful at the Directed Energy Lab. Because I could write code, I used multiple automated processes to continually test the security of the environment where so much classified information was stored. Essentially, I attacked my own network (now termed a "penetration test") regularly to find vulnerabilities that could be exploited.

Some of the biggest problems there, though, came from within. Many issues surfaced surrounding the determination of who really owned the data, the researcher or the government. Too often at that time, the government lost the battle because the research was being copied to multiple locations and different kinds of media, even presumably kept off-site. This battle was eventually decided with controls put in place sometime after my departure.

I led a couple of people at the Directed Energy Lab: one was a pure academic at heart, and the other had more of a hands-on persona. The two together brought different skill sets to the table, and as it turned out, their skills were complementary for the objectives we had to achieve.

My time at the Directed Energy Lab was filled with wonderful experiences and challenges that were truly difficult. I began to really see that people naturally have different traits and capabilities (positive and negative) and that the key to overcoming problems more holistically might be to identify those traits in each person and put the right pieces together to form a cohesive team. Easy to say, hard to do.

After a year of applying for multiple management jobs within CACI, it really seemed that there was no real upward mobility, making the goals within my career plan unachievable without moving to a different company. I was supervising people, yet I was being compensated as an individual contributor. Because I was in a contract position, I was a resource specific to that contract. They could not move me, even if they'd wanted to.

Consulting – Management Techniques

Shortly after Sprint acquired a company called Paranet, which was actively growing their consulting group, the telecom giant posted a position for a project manager in San Antonio, Texas. It appeared to be a good fit and would allow me to gain experience in managing both people and resources and a path to advance in the organization.

I began my tenure at Sprint Paranet managing multiple projects and supporting the sales team in their quest to sign new business. Through the next six months, I learned a lot, refining my understanding of resource management.

Lesson Learned:
Managing human capital is not the same as leading people.

I found that resource management, by definition, is about managing the schedules and budgets for people, projects, equipment, and supplies. What I learned during this period was that management of human capital (the skills, knowledge, and experience possessed by an individual or population, viewed in terms of their value or cost to an organization) is very different from leading people, and in large organizations, even today, leaders unfortunately forget that fact.

Lesson Learned:
Listening to people is an art, not a science, and to be successful you must be able to listen.

Although "integrity" and "diversity" are nice buzzwords, "Lead by Example" is the most important among leadership values. It transcends cultures and works in autocratic environments as well as collaborative ones. My opportunity to lead teams as a project manager was more about the classic management of resources, but I chose to be more of a hands-on leader and work with the people that were on the team. My goal was to take an interest in their opinions and

> **Lesson Learned:**
> Lead by example – ensure that you are doing the same things, following the same processes, or executing on the same values that you are telling, directing, or suggesting the employees must follow, execute, or implement.

> **Lesson Learned:**
> Continually evaluate your leadership capabilities and adjust when needed.

ideas while doing my best to ensure that I was setting a good example of how to lead, not just manage.

This sort of self-review starts with evaluation (a couple of times a year is a good frequency) to ensure that you are looking at yourself in a critical way and, where needed, making changes to your leadership style. Be consistent, but be flexible enough to adjust based on the business environment or culture you find yourself in. For example, my style was much more directorial than my peers, and within the culture of Sprint, I had to change my style to engage with the employees for better results.

After demonstrating my value to the company, I was promoted to service delivery manager (SDM) in November 1998 and continued that role until December 1999. During this time, I had many more opportunities for self-reflection and to improve my resource management capabilities. Most importantly, though, I developed my consulting approach and refined the way I interacted with clients.

> **Lesson Learned:**
> Listen to the client, understand their needs (requirements), and determine what business outcome they are looking for.

The ability to understand client needs and requirements became one of the cornerstones of my development as a civilian leader. I learned how to focus on listening to clients, not just what they said but how they articulated their needs, and asked the right questions to determine their desired business outcome. This process had a direct impact on sales, helping improve the ratio of client meetings to signed contracts. It's a metric that I'm not sure is really valuable, but Sprint tied it to revenue growth.

Chapter 4: CISO: Leading the Charge

Management and Leadership, Two Different Things

Adjusting Within Corporate Cultures

In 1999, most of my peers were vice presidents or held some equivalent title and were earning a significantly higher salary than I was. I was still so far behind, my career plan had to be accelerated. Because the path to upward mobility at Sprint Paranet was clear, I knew that the length of time to earn higher positions was much longer than I was willing to accept.

Since I had improved my management ability and made some adjustments to my leadership style, I was really ready to move into a more challenging role. So, in December 1999, I accepted a position with a technology consulting firm called Enterprise Networking Systems (ENS). Shortly after I joined, it went public and changed its name to Netigy.

My initial position was as a consulting services manager (CSM), but I quickly moved into a joint role as a senior principal consultant, maintaining my management role and leveraging my technical capabilities and experience with clients. My leadership style had to be adjusted to the corporate culture, but I also started noticing that my peers knew a whole lot about management and not much about leadership.

As a Marine, leadership was ingrained and management was a by-product. Management can be defined as:

> *the act or art of managing; the conducting or supervising of something (such as a business).*
>
> or
>
> *the act or manner of managing; handling, direction, or control.*

Either definition brings me to the point that management is generally about resources such as equipment, facilities, and supplies. This was what a vast majority of my colleagues at that time believed was leadership. I could not get them to understand that leadership is about people.

Even in the most basic scenario, leadership is defined as "the action of leading a group of people or an organization."

> **Lesson Learned:** Make a concerted effort to understand your direct reports, both professionally and personally – it will pay dividends down the road.

My personal definition is a bit more complicated, but it's been engineered from my collective experience, plus the opinions and attitudes of the many strong leadership mentors in my career, both military and civilian.

My definition? Leadership is the art of motivating a group of people to act toward achieving a common goal and the science of combining your personality traits and leadership skills that compel others to want to follow your direction.

Leveraging a Startup Culture

Netigy provided me with plenty of opportunities to expand my skill set. For example, I was given the chance to speak in public at conferences, on panels, at luncheons, and in various forums where information security was discussed. My contact list grew explosively. As my organization grew, I had to implement regular face-to-face meetings so that the team members could get to know each other, fostering collaboration within the region.

In a services company, it really is all about the people who make the work possible. Their excitement, their experience, their relationships, and their satisfaction are vital to customer happiness.

I was starting to check all my boxes again and felt like I was catching up to my peers, but most importantly, I was having fun going to work every day. Leading seven people was a familiar effort, but managing resources like equipment and transportation was a true challenge. Because my team was spread across six states, my most important job was to ensure that they had what they needed to deliver to the clients.

I had a lot of work to do on resource management, but I had the good fortune to exercise the leadership principles that had been ingrained during the twenty years before this assignment.

I still use the same leadership principles today. They are:

- *Know yourself and seek self-improvement.*
- *Be technically and tactically proficient.*
- *Develop a sense of responsibility among your subordinates.*

- *Make sound and timely decisions.*
- *Set the example.*
- *Know your people and look out for their welfare.*
- *Keep your people informed.*
- *Seek responsibility and take responsibility for your actions.*
- *Ensure assigned tasks are understood, supervised, and accomplished.*
- *Train your people as a team.*
- *Utilize your organization in accordance with its capabilities.*

Although I have added to and massaged these a bit, they have become the foundation upon which every leadership decision I make is based. Every leader has traits that are their undeniable signatures – even bad ones.

Whether or not I had mastered all the leadership traits I admire most, my challenge became conveying them to my team members as they worked to hone their own leadership styles. The best leaders have fully developed these traits:

- **Dependability.** *The certainty of proper performance of duty.*
- **Bearing.** *The ability to create a favorable impression in carriage, appearance, and personal conduct at all times.*
- **Courage.** *The mental quality that recognizes fear of danger or criticism but enables a person to proceed in the face of it with calmness and firmness.*

- **Decisiveness.** *The ability to make decisions promptly and to announce them in a clear, confident manner.*
- **Endurance.** *The mental and physical stamina measured by the ability to withstand pain, fatigue, stress, and hardship.*
- **Enthusiasm.** *The display of sincere interest and exuberance in the performance of duty.*
- **Initiative.** *The drive to take action in the absence of orders.*
- **Integrity.** *Uprightness of character and soundness of moral principles, including the qualities of truthfulness and honesty.*
- **Judgment.** *The ability to weigh facts and possible solutions on which to base sound decisions.*
- **Justice.** *The ability to give reward and punishment according to the merits of the case in question and to administer the system impartially and consistently.*
- **Knowledge.** *Understanding of a science or an art. The range of one's information, including professional knowledge and an understanding of your people.*
- **Tact.** *The ability to deal with others without creating offense.*
- **Unselfishness.** *Avoidance of providing for one's own comfort and personal advancement at the expense of others.*
- **Loyalty.** *The quality of faithfulness to one's seniors, subordinates, and peers.*

> **Lesson Learned:**
> *Not everyone wants to be a Leader, but everyone has some of the leadership traits inside of them.*

> **Lesson Learned:**
> *Don't focus on the next shiny object without understanding what makes it shine. It is never greener grass on the other side of the mountain.*

I believe that the primary mission of all leaders is to help make our people better leaders themselves, rather than expecting them to be "yes" people. Having the chance to mold the next generation of leaders at Netigy became the source of the greatest satisfaction in my civilian career to date.

Nothing lasts forever, though, and in May 2001, I heard about a company that was expanding and looking for a person to assume the position of General Manager, Director of Security. I accepted the job that year and started juggling the management of several consultants, driving new business, and delivering various assessment services.

I was in this position on September 11, 2001, one of the most tragic days in United States history. Anyone who was an adult, and many who weren't yet, remember where they were and what they were doing when they heard that the Twin Towers in New York had been attacked. I firmly believe that September 11 was a modern version of Pearl Harbor for so many people.

Of course, after the shock passed, my brain snapped into action. Was anyone from my team working or living in New York? No? Did I know anyone working in the Towers? What could I do to help the effort there? Luckily, no one on my team was in New York, but I did lose several friends on that dark day.

Events like these cause us to reflect and assess our lives – it is human nature, I believe – but they can't help us see the future any more clearly. As a direct consequence, for example, I lost my job in November 2001 as a part of the tragedy's aftermath. It was the first time I had ever been unemployed (and hopefully the last).

Lesson Learned: Always try to turn a negative situation into a positive situation.

When these types of actions occur, you should take advantage of them however you can. I went back to school to pursue an MBA. Why not? I had the time.

Expanding My Experience Base – CISO Development

The First CISO Job

While working on a Master of Business Administration with an Information Systems emphasis, I was approached by the University of Texas Health Science Center at San Antonio with a job offer. After a detailed interview process, I accepted an offer as the first Chief Information Security Officer for the Health Science Center in February 2002.

Although I took a substantial cut in pay from my previous position in the consulting world, this would be my first assignment as a CISO. The latter was the primary reason for my acceptance, and although the pay was not on level with my previous position, the job was a critical step up. Based on my career plan at the time, I had finally caught up to my peers, at least from a leadership position perspective.

My new role required me to build a staff and create an information-security program that would be a differentiator in the academic healthcare industry. The first obstacle I identified was that everything was done by consensus management, but, given that this was an academic environment, it was simply the culture. The second was that the idea of controls (of any kind) was in opposition to the learning environment where openness and sharing were crucial to collaboration.

Each member of my team had a unique skill set with strengths that complemented the team as a whole. This was the first time I actually matched team members based on skill set, personalities, education, culture, and discipline. It is important to note that I already had people assigned that were in positions before I took over as the CISO. They were inherently my baseline. I brought additional people to the team, but with careful consideration, the balance of strengths and weaknesses were maintained.

> **Lesson Learned:** Don't throw the baby out with the bath water. Everyone has potential and can contribute; you as a leader must figure out what those skills are, highlight them, and mentor each person to be better.

Opportunity Knocks

I graduated with my MBA in May 2004. At that point, I had successfully designed, implemented, and managed an information-security program; it was time to take the next step and apply myself to something larger.

I started putting feelers out regarding opportunities in San Antonio for CISOs, and there were several interesting opportunities that were publicized. One evening, I was at a United Way promotions dinner where major companies in San Antonio got together to raise money and share ideas to raise awareness about the United Way's capabilities.

I sat at a table with the Health Science Center President. His wife brought over the CEO and President of Clarke American and introduced me. This meeting (although brief and probably not memorable to him), was

> **Lesson Learned:**
> *You never know when a chance meeting becomes an incredible opportunity – always be prepared.*

the start of my ten-year run at what is now Harland Clarke Holdings Corp.

The day after that fateful introduction, I received an email from Clarke American Recruiting asking me if I might be interested in the Executive Director and CISO position that was now vacant.

Unbelievable!

I was so excited that I answered almost immediately. Yes, absolutely, I would be interested! After nine interviews (seven individual and two panel) I was offered the job; after just two days of consideration, I accepted.

For about 45 days, I did both jobs – CISO for UTHSCSA and CISO for Clarke American – and officially joined Clarke American in August 2004. I called this my "dream job" because:

- *The job paid well, and the benefits were very good*
- *I was given the opportunity to build a program*
- *I had the honor to lead people*
- *There were all kinds of challenges*
- *I exceeded my personal plan*

Over an eight-year period, Clarke American was acquired and became Harland Clarke. The new entity went public, acquired multiple companies, divested, and returned to private holding, expanded internationally to India and Europe, and became the second largest check manufacturer and a key financial service provider for many financial institutions.

The changes that the people at the company were asked to endure were many, but the leadership was solid and the teams survived. We all learned a vast amount about business during this eight-year epoch, including many things that are not taught in a classroom but can only be mastered by doing.

What a great opportunity it was!

International Exposure

Based on my worldwide travels (primarily in the military), the company knew I was the right person to trek to India and Europe to manage security-related projects globally. I made multiple trips myself, but I also sent my team members to these facilities so they could both travel and gain some international experience. By exposing them to our own business in India specifically, and potential outsourcing businesses in India, I felt like they would be better prepared to compete in the global economy.

I also began a lot of travel to various places, from India (multiple locations including Chennai and Trivandrum), to the Philippines (Manila) and Norway, as well as Japan. Although my previous travel experience was useful, commercial travel was much easier than military transport.

This part of the business experience led me to other hands-on education like learning about the cultures that we were about to engage on a more permanent basis. I also learned some valuable lessons about outsourcing, most notably that outsourcing does not necessarily improve the bottom line.

Be leery of outsourcing. It almost makes better business sense to buy or build a company in a different country than to outsource to any of the large outsourcing contractors.

From a security perspective, it was difficult at best to ensure that the supply chain was following all the prescriptive security controls and not taking shortcuts. This certainly applied to other functional areas such as quality and safety. Large Information Communications Technology (ICT) companies were generally solid partners, but quality in some of those companies left a little to be desired.

Lesson Learned:
Cultural diversity is a great thing that can be a game changer and part of the value statement for the company.

I'm most proud of being able to help my people understand that cultural diversity was a valuable asset and that we (Americans) need to embrace and learn about other cultures as we expand our businesses into multiple countries around the globe.

Now a vice president and Chief Information Security Officer, I was able to give back to the community and grew my team from one to eight. I also implemented a Managed Security Service Provider (MSSP) to extend my security operations. Things were running very smoothly, and I had time to do other things.

A couple of colleagues and I founded the Security Leaders Forum, which brought leaders to the table to talk, share information, and provide thought leadership on security-related topics. I also did more speaking engagements at various conferences, summits, and forums, mostly to evangelize the information-security programs and get the attention of business executives.

As we continued to grow the company, an opportunity to take on a new role appeared. The job title was Senior Vice President of Infrastructure and Chief Information Security Strategist. What it meant was that I was responsible for leading technology innovations and infrastructure changes, as well as providing strategic advice to the Chief Security Officer. At this point I led about 45 people and managed an IT service provider of approximately 200 people.

The new post was a change of pace, and, while it was not part of my plan, I adjusted accordingly and integrated it into the bigger picture. I really wanted to get to the Holy Grail for security executives – Global Chief Information Security Officer at an international conglomerate.

After spending a fantastic 10 years and one month with Harland Clarke, knowing that I had an impact on the success of the company and the growth of multiple team members allowed me to look to the next thing without regret. I really thrived there; it was one of the most rewarding stints I spent at a civilian corporation.

Chapter 5: Managing Your Own Business

The Challenge

As leaders, we often fail to teach our team members about finances and help them attain financial literacy. Even though high schools and colleges are teaching math and science, they are failing future workers by not teaching fundamental skills that every person needs to have in their toolbox. Career planning and financial planning are crucial.

One of the goals of my career plan was to become financially independent. My primary reasoning, of course, was that I didn't want to be dependent on anyone. But as important, I did not want to be put in a position where I had to be beholden to my employer.

> **Lesson Learned:**
> *You can speak your mind and provide honest and accurate (unfiltered) advice or recommendations, and you can walk away from a job if you do not agree with the company's direction or strategy.*

I was able to finally become financially independent while at Harland Clarke (and it's a refreshing position to be in). I gave my notice to a wonderful company that allowed me to grow and supported me fully, then took some time off. There was no need to have a place to go, and after giving 100 percent every day, unplugging for a month was exhilarating.

I must tell you that after a month, though, I wanted to get back to work, to do something.

I started my own business to fill that void, but also to share my expertise with small-business leaders and fuel my passion for information security. I could choose exactly which projects I wanted to do and had the freedom to turn down those that I couldn't support. I continued to speak at conferences and forums and support local information-security organizations.

As I took on new business, I created additional relationships both regionally and nationally, and expanded my interactions with various executives across multiple vertical industries. My amassed knowledge reached more business leaders through informative articles and input to various publications.

Legalities

Creating your own business is much easier today with the range of digital materials available, the ability to get legal advice right away, automations for tasks like bookkeeping, and online personas that can help establish your presence. From start to finish, it took me approximately one month to set a company up and begin to provide services.

The most difficult parts of the process for me were making the fundamental decisions of what kind of legal structure I wanted based on tax rules and state laws and what services or products I was going to sell. Certainly, I had to put my business book knowledge to the test and live and breathe my MBA.

The individual services I finally settled on were strategic advisory and assessment services. Most of my clients were small businesses, although there were a couple of mid-size companies that had requirements that I could meet. Having very low overhead and the ability to adjust my own pricing was a huge advantage against bigger competitors.

My biggest issue was volume. I couldn't take on a lot of work at once unless I hired additional staff, and that is such a balancing act. Revenue recognition and bookings that were accurate was another challenge, as was determining whether to bring on another employee or use a contractor. These were all critical decisions in the expansion discussion.

Lesson Learned: Automate support functions as much as possible but continue the human interaction.

As for the legal structure of my company, The Petrie Group, I went with the C-Corp. It allows for the following advantages under Texas law:

- *Separate legal identity*
- *Limited liability for the owners*
- *Perpetual existence*
- *Separation between ownership and management*
- *No restrictions on who can hold shares*
- *Readily transferable shares*
- *Well-established legal precedents*
- *Widespread acceptance by venture capitalists and other investors*
- *Ability to offer stock options*
- *Tax planning opportunities*

Some would argue that a Limited Liability Company (LLC) would be a better way to go, but when I looked at where I intended to go in the future, the C-Corp was a better solution for me, with the ability to offer stock options and to have a perpetual existence.

I consulted with multiple small businesses throughout the startup process and was able to meet my delivery requirements and payroll. Given the small size of my company, command and control was simple and streamlined, and costs remained under control as I took on more business.

Cookie-cutter security assessments were my primary service offering. They were valuable but an easier sell for small businesses than for large ones. As inquiries from larger companies began to come in, there was a need for customization of both the scope of the assessment and the delivery of the report. Adjustments had to be made to meet expectations.

Perhaps most importantly, the company gave me a wonderful opportunity to mentor several cybersecurity professionals who have become solid leaders and go-to professionals in the individual security disciplines in their own right. Mentorship was, and still is, a rewarding part of my professional life. The feeling that you're helping real people and have an ability to make a positive impact on the future of your profession is indescribable.

Independence

As I met with various companies needing help with cybersecurity issues, it became very clear that there was (and is) a lack of leadership at the middle management level and above. It doesn't appear that we're teaching our young professionals how to lead people; even large companies seem to be failing in this regard.

We continue to do a good job in teaching them how to manage assets and resources, but not to lead people. We are also not teaching our people how to leverage their own experiences to turn negatives into positives.

Some of it may go back to financial literacy. When I was having discussions with my colleagues, I found too often that they were so afraid of losing their job because of the financial impact that they failed to take chances, to innovate, and to lead.

My advice (for whatever it was worth) was to create a plan that included simple strategies like "pay yourself first" and dollar cost averaging so that they could take care of their futures while they still had the tools to do so.

You can't be bold, a risk taker, and an innovator without being in a secure financial position first. In some cases, these managers were so busy protecting their jobs that they forgot to do their jobs. They didn't lead their people.

Since I had achieved (and exceeded) my career goals and my children were now adults on their own in the world, it was time to start planning the next twenty years. There were still challenges yet to conquer, and there were still lots of things I wanted to do, including becoming a board member, holding a membership on certain councils, and making even more impact on our young professionals.

During late September 2014, I started receiving inquiries regarding my availability to take on various jobs at different companies. It was nice to be asked, but what was really happening was that I was on one or more lists of qualified CISOs and security executives that recruiters used to fill job positions.

Lesson Learned:
In order to be competitive for any job, you first must be on that hiring manager's list, the boss's list, or the recruiter's list to even be considered.

A call from a colleague at IBM (Big Blue) came through during the first week in October 2014. Although I had many job offers since I left Harland Clarke in August 2014, this was the first with some real potential and would allow me to explore new challenges in my career.

Chapter 6: The IBM Experience – Briefing Boards of Directors

Big Blue in Action

A colleague from IBM proposed we meet over coffee to talk about where IBM was going to go next regarding their security division. As explained to me at the time, IBM was planning to separate its security-related business and bring together all its security assets and resources to form a section that would be accountable for cybersecurity services across the spectrum of IBM products and services.

This was an interesting approach, but I had to wonder why they hadn't done this consolidation when they acquired Internet Security Systems (ISS) and the X-Force component. It was the perfect opportunity to create a security business unit and remove solutions and services from the product division.

My friend explained that they had been planning this move for years and were just now ready to pull the trigger.

I would be part of creating a real cybersecurity company underneath one of the most acclaimed brands in the world. I accepted a position as an executive consultant in IBM's consulting division. IBM was reorganizing and truly making the effort to bring the security-related organizations together under one unit. What a fantastic opportunity to be part of business history!

It was exciting to provide input for this endeavor. There's a ton of talent and thought leadership at IBM – no question – but I don't think that IBM totally embraced the concept of "security by design" in their internal security program. Their strategic consulting division was also stifled by the company's need to attach everything they do to product (and let's not forget commission-stacking).

Their products have always been solid and secure, in my opinion, especially their mainframe architecture, and the Z-series has been phenomenal from a secure platform perspective. But history has taught us what corporations should not do when they acquire a pure-play security company. A few examples that come to mind immediately include:

- IBM acquisition of Internet Security Systems (ISS) (2006)
- BT acquisition of Counterpane Internet Security (2006)
- Verizon acquisition of Cybertrust (2007)
- Intel acquisition of McAfee (2011)
- NTT acquisition of Solutionary (2013)

At the end of the day, corporations make business decisions based on what they believe to be facts and ultimately what is in the best interest of their shareholders and clients. Any leader you talk to will tell you that they make many mistakes, but they hope that the good decisions outweigh the bad ones and that their goals and objectives were attained.

If you analyze the above examples, a lot of

disappointment and failure was caused by the desire to put a square peg in a round hole. I think in the cases of BT and Verizon, they really wanted their security companies to be treated as commodities and forced them to move into their telecom pricing models. They also wanted to leverage the telecom customer model (little or no touch points and limited relationship building) to integrate the services and solutions into their commission stack.

The problem is that the security business is about trust and people, and so far, only relying on tech or managing by SKUs has not worked. IBM, on the other hand, acquired ISS in 2006, and it took nine years for their leadership to determine that they needed to create and go to market with a stand-alone security business that could become the premier cybersecurity company in the world.

The Idea

When I came on board at IBM, leadership was moving very quickly after what I can only guess was an eight-year planning exercise. The idea, and what sold me, was that experienced leaders with information and data-security backgrounds were going to build a business that was focused on the full security life cycle with services and solutions that were client-focused, not necessarily IBM-product-focused.

My job was to work with various company executives (by vertical industry) and conduct strategic assessments that would identify gaps. I would also provide recommendations to those same executives about cybersecurity and the business outcomes that their security executive was trying to achieve. I was also tasked with presenting to Boards of Directors (BoDs) the actionable recommendations that would:

- *Reduce their risks and their exposure*
- *Communicate the technical security solutions in business terms and business outcomes*
- *Discuss security as an enabler and a differentiator*

My experience with BoDs was only through exposure to my own BoD in the past. Now I was the expert presenting to BoDs with different levels of maturity and experience relating to cybersecurity. In some cases, they had no exposure to security issues whatsoever, and until recently, board members with cybersecurity backgrounds or experience were few and far between.

Lesson Learned:
When presenting or briefing a board, you must do your homework and understand where each member of the board's background is relating to security, as well as where you may need to focus additional time for an individual member to understand the topic.

Looking Inside

As a leader in your chosen field, you must be able to go to the Board with credibility and then be prepared to make your case in ten minutes, then provide time for questions from individual members. Always plan for 30 minutes unless you have been given a specific time frame for your presentation/ discussion.

Going into a Board setting armed with a slide deck with 50 slides is not the approach I recommend. Board Members are becoming more mature, and they certainly are not looking for a sales pitch. Clarity, directness, discussion, and active listening are the key attributes required to accomplish the job. If you need slides, graphical support slides work best, and linking the data with business outcomes is highly recommended.

As I honed my skills and was more comfortable in my own delivery capability, I found that the leadership principles I outlined in earlier chapters were relevant in these strategic discussions and helped me tune my delivery to the needs of Board leaders.

Spending more time in the IBM culture revealed that the talented leaders did not do as much mentoring as needed; senior leadership spent more of their available cycles on specific people who they thought would be helpful to them in their pursuit of their success. I understand you can't boil the ocean, and a leader has only limited time available; however, a lot of the members of management that I interacted with were concerned only with their individual achievements and not the people who would be the next generation of leaders.

I had the opportunity to work with a very small number of security professionals who, as a team, assessed the IBM internal security program. They were leaders from different departments within IBM, and I chose to use the opportunity to observe them in their unfiltered environments. I'd then take those observations and use them as teaching points for the team I was working with, pointing out both the positives and the negatives.

I provided constructive criticism where I thought it might be valuable to specific leaders, and I felt like most took the information and made some positive adjustments. At the same time, I also listened to their perspectives

> **Lesson Learned:**
> *Do not be afraid to provide criticism and thoughts to individual leaders if they are constructive.*

regarding leadership and the way forward for IBM. I, too, used some of their insight to adjust my leadership style and approach.

Members of an organization, especially those in leadership roles, shouldn't be afraid to provide criticism and thoughts to individual leaders, provided those comments are constructive. What is not constructive is framing comments as bullying or being forcefully abusive with the communication.

This type of behavior is unacceptable and never, ever stands the test of time. To be clear, I did not see that kind of behavior during my assessment of the internal security program, but I did observe this behavior at some of the client sites I supported. When you encounter this type of leadership style, I strongly recommend that you use it as an example of bad leadership.

Deflation of the Idea

The IBM experience (like anything else) when executed as taught, is an extremely powerful consulting methodology. I believe it has a positive impact on the success of companies.

Overall, I had great opportunities to build relationships with CEOs and their staffs, as well as trade ideas about leading people, managing resources, attaining goals, and providing shareholder value. There were important processes that I learned while in this position, but the most valuable equity that came from this position were the additional contacts and new relationships built with clients and internal staff at IBM.

As the end of 2015 approached, it appeared that the security experiment was done. The people who were instrumental in breaking out the security services and solutions into a stand-alone company were leaving as quickly as they came, and my internal colleagues were whispering that security was going back into the product organization.

Other signs started to appear. Consultants began to drop their notices of resignation, and there was a shortage of personnel to deliver on projects that were already sold. At the same time, the CISO, the Security Business Leader, and multiple other key staff were departing without warning. There was not a lot of communication about what was going to happen next and what impact it would have on the employees who remained.

Lesson Learned: Always have a plan B and C ready to go. If the worst-case scenario happens and there's a reduction in force or a cadre of people get fired, you will already have a plan in place to execute if needed.

The writing appeared to be on the wall. The X-Force would remain, but the individual components of the fledgling security business were doomed to move back into product. I think things would have been different if there had been a more targeted approach to communicating to the employees who may have been affected.

Lesson Learned: Crisp communication is essential to manage change and employee expectations; if change is occurring all around them, employees will come to various conclusions on their own.

The outcome of a lack of communication is always worse than if management put out a concise communication. If an incomplete motion picture is produced and the communication about the portion of the story that remains has gone out and is unclear, the potential audience will make up an ending for the picture. Spoiler alert: it's usually a horror story, not a happy ending.

Chapter 7: Global CISO – Things You Don't Learn from a Book

Always Be Ready to Walk Through an Open Door

Dinners Are Never Just Dinners

In December 2015, I was completing a project in Chicago (working for IBM) when I received an email from the CEO of Solutionary, asking me how I was doing and where I was in the world. As we exchanged emails, he told me he was just getting back from Tokyo, was heading to Chicago, and would be in town for a couple of days. He invited me to dinner with the intent to catch up on what each of us had been doing since the last time we talked.

Certainly it would be good to chat, and we scheduled a dinner meeting toward the end of the week, before I was scheduled to head back home. This turned out to be a significant change in direction for me and set the stage for what would be an interesting transition. I have always said that it was the best steak dinner I ever had.

We talked for three hours, and he answered all my questions, and it was refreshing. It was somewhat overwhelming, but in a positive way. Make no mistake, it was an interview. Chance meetings, impromptu dinners, drinks, anything that is face to face, I believe that there are alternative agendas. No book (besides this one) will tell you that you should always be prepared and never let your guard down when it comes to opportunity. If there is one, I never read it.

I firmly believe that dinner meeting was more than just dinner. Whether intentional or not, it was the beginning of a working relationship that, in my mind, was the start of my training to be an international executive. It became my launching pad for a position as CISO for Solutionary.

> **Lesson Learned:**
> When a door is opened, you must be prepared to walk through it – but do so with open eyes and reasonable expectations.

Negotiate! Everything's on the Table Until It's Not

In January, after several interviews and a face-to-face meeting at the company headquarters, I was offered the job. Ten days later, I signed the offer letter.

As I transitioned into my new position as CISO, it was essential for me to understand the culture of the company. Acquired in 2015, Solutionary was still in a state of change and with new ownership, but also with a true integration on the horizon. Communication the new strategy and direction appeared to be sound and frequent.

If you recall in Chapter 4, I stated that, "I really wanted to get to the Holy Grail for security executives – Global Chief Information Security Officer at an international conglomerate." Well, that was still on the radar screen, and it was what my plan listed as my end goal.

In late January, as I was creating my roadmap for a new, strategic Information Security Program, I had the opportunity to meet the CFO/CIO of NTT Group (NTT Holdings), who spent a few minutes with me discussing the next evolution in the transformation of the security companies of NTT. Interestingly enough, he talked about a Global CISO position within the consolidated company and asked if I was interested in that type of position.

Of course I was!

Knowing that NTT was planning to create a new company, I shifted priorities a bit, continuing with a short-term strategy (for the existing company) and forming a second long-term strategy for the new global company. This ultimately would require changes in direction and some consolidation of staff.

My original team was two people, but in February 2016 we moved the physical security team to my organization, which added four more workers. The team was limited in their experience with global operations, so some shifting would be needed to balance the scale.

At the same time, my second-in-command decided to resign and move to another company. I started to notice a shift in the security professional landscape, making this skill set an extremely marketable one.

Lesson Learned:
Where possible, bring former employees who are trustworthy and loyal to work for you. You are served better with people who understand your work ethic and your philosophies.

There were all kinds of security positions open, and people were not tied down to local companies if they were able to travel and work from home. Security professionals were commanding higher salaries as well. Given that these transformational changes were clearly coming, I shifted my priorities to building a new team. In April, I brought on a former colleague to be the Director of Information Security Operations to replace my departing right hand.

Always Be Prepared

I had a follow-up chat with the NTT CFO/CIO regarding the Global CISO position he had mentioned, and he confirmed they would need one for the new Company. A month later, I was summoned to Tokyo to participate in a series of R&D meetings. I had no idea what to expect (or how to prepare) for the series of meetings in Tokyo. Luckily, I had a 13-hour plane flight to assess the situation, research the people, and put together a high-level strategy for responding to questions that I anticipated would be asked.

What I didn't know at the time was that I was being interviewed for a newly created Global Information Security Officer position for the newly integrated security company made from the old NTT.

About a week after returning from the Tokyo trip, I was officially informed that I was now designated as the Global CISO and would be appointed to the new company's executive team. I began to execute a personnel plan and hired an additional information-security professional in the United States. I also began the interview process for regional CISOs across the world to support our new global structure, primarily looking at personnel inside the entire NTT Group organization.

The organizational structure was announced internally for the new company, NTT Security, in July. I prioritized my objectives and gained approval for budget, personnel, policy, organization, and strategy – all of which were approved by August 1, the official incorporation date of NTT Security.

I didn't have any book references to fall back on because this was totally new territory I was embarking on. There were certainly case studies (as mentioned in previous chapters) but nothing that would serve as a successful template for what NTTS was aiming to accomplish.

NTTS, the new company, was created from the integration of legacy companies that NTT had purchased and operated independently; those included Solutionary, Integralis, NTT Com Security, and Earthwave. I needed to consolidate all the internal security resources and restructure them into regional components. NTT also implemented a matrix-style management structure that was new to the organization (at least the U.S. component), which further complicated the integration both culturally and organizationally.

A Regional Structure for a Global Company

Restructuring and Growing Pains

NTTS corporate had decided that we would govern globally but deliver regionally, which required a regional CISO structure. I had anticipated this decision and was already moving in a direction to ensure this happened flawlessly. In support of the integration activity, I reduced my staff by one person (in August) due to redundant roles that I had identified in July.

For those who agree that security services is a people business, terminating an employee is one of the most difficult decisions you (as a leader) deal with. That's why I have a simple rule for this: always execute a termination yourself.

Don't staff it out, don't let a human resources person handle it, don't do it by phone. Conduct the termination of a staff member yourself, in person, and be prepared to provide an explanation. Certainly, you should have a member of HR in the room to support you, and perhaps someone from legal, depending on the circumstances, but you must take ownership of the decision.

> **Lesson Learned:** Always execute a termination yourself. Don't staff it out, don't let a human resources person handle it, don't do it by phone. Conduct the termination of a person yourself, in person, and be prepared to provide an explanation. Certainly, you should have an HR person in the room to support you, and perhaps a legal person depending on the circumstances, but you must take ownership of the decision.

Why is this so important? Because the decision to fire someone is personal and directly impacts lives, well beyond the person involved. Their family, friends, and co-workers are also affected directly by this level of change.

I can tell you that people who I have terminated, months and years after, told me they appreciated that I personally informed them of their dismissal and that I ensured they understood the circumstances that drove the decision.

This was of some comfort as I moved through my career. Hopefully it will be to you, as well.

Strengths and Weaknesses

On August 1, 2016, NTT Security was officially a company and publicly announced worldwide. By August 30, I had new leaders in place and staff to support them. There were four Regional CISOs covering the Americas (Canada, U.S., Central America, and South America), EMEA (Europe, Middle East, and

Africa), APAC (Asia Pacific), and Japan. In September 2016, I brought my staff together to review the global strategy, move forward with any adjustments, and finalize budgets for the coming fiscal year, which ran from March to February.

My CISOs were diverse: British, Australian, American, and Japanese. The designated language that NTT Security had chosen to use was International English. This made communications a bit easier, although we had to adjust for our Japanese colleague and ensure that we had some translation capability.

It is critical that you as a leader get to know your direct reports, what their backgrounds are, their family constructs, their individual cultures, and everything, really, that makes them tick. It's also so important that you become familiar with their capabilities and their weaknesses as you move forward with integrating and consolidating personnel across the globe.

Life Lesson:
People make teams work – they are like puzzle pieces; you must find the right pieces that form the perfect picture. The more you know and understand your leaders, the better you can fit the pieces together.

This is where a lot of the lessons scattered throughout this book come together. You, as a leader, must bring out the best in your people. And when you build a team, those team members must become a cohesive unit. Each person has certain capabilities and qualities, as well as certain weaknesses and faults. When you create a team, recognize that each individual becomes a puzzle piece that should fit with others to form a clear picture; each can feed off the others to compensate for internal weaknesses.

The Politics of It All

I believe we were a successful team as we navigated new territory as a new company. By November, my staff grew to 12 people located around the globe. We now had both a Data Protection Officer/Privacy Officer and a Global Systems Security Audit Manager.

The first thing I advise an American Global CISO for an international or multinational corporation is to check your ego at the door. Take advantage of cultural diversity and ideas that come with it and always listen and continue to learn from your colleagues. If you position yourself as a trusted advisor, the political landscape is a bit easier to navigate. Try not to connect yourself to a single person in the chain of command; you never know when a person will fall from favor in an international conglomerate.

The phrase "keep your friends close and your enemies closer" applies double; always be aware that all people are not transparent, nor do they have your best interest in mind. This doesn't mean that you should be uncooperative, condescending, or confrontational, it simply means being cognizant of your organizational dynamics and the people that are in positions of leadership. Learn to navigate the political minefield carefully.

It's also vital to understand who the major influencers are within the organization at the highest levels. As I navigated through the transformation and the company politics at NTTS, I found that constructive change was not only necessary but beneficial to the organization. It provided the information

> **Lesson Learned:**
> *Things are not chiseled in stone – you can change direction. You must lead change and manage the expectation of change.*

people needed to make their own decisions.

The key is that leaders must over-communicate change, not try to hide it or let a major change appear without any warning. This concept was put to the test when leadership at NTTS decided that they were going to reorganize the supporting functions as global organizations versus regional ones.

For me, it wasn't a huge issue. I saw very little change, moving from five direct reports to eight and making some adjustments regarding contractors and other service provider functions. I was able to organically cut costs while keeping my existing personnel and increasing by two full-time employees.

I was charged with managing the following areas in our global infrastructure: Information Security Management System (ISMS); Cybersecurity Operations; Vendor Risk Management; Governance, Risk, and Compliance (GRC); Data Protection/Privacy; Security Audit; and Business Continuity. This new organizational structure became effective April 1, 2018, just two years after the formation of NTTS.

> **Lesson Learned:**
> *Do your best to do the right thing every time. This expands on several previous lessons that I have learned over the years, and sometimes the right thing is not the most popular thing.*

Communication to the teams globally became crucial, and overcommunication was the rule. Monthly all-hands staff meetings and weekly direct report meetings were the norm as we navigated the business changes that were being implemented.

Continuing to Navigate the Changes

In any company, regardless of size or location, I think it is important for a Global CISO to build up political capital as they implement their overall security strategy. This is not as easy as it sounds, and you don't want to focus on this issue – primarily because you could very well alienate your peers if they believe you're self-promoting and only looking out for number one.

Political capital can be gained simply by doing the right thing and providing 120 percent of support to the leader's decisions. Having said that, it doesn't mean you should become a yes-person. What it means is that you provide constructive feedback (and in some cases constructive criticism) to your leader and realize that once the leader has considered the input and made a decision, you must support that decision. This gains trust and confidence without showboating.

If you can't come to a place where you can support your leader's decision, you probably need to think about leaving the company and finding a new company that you can support. Your beliefs may be in massive conflict with the company's base philosophy, and that's ok – it's just not meant to be.

As a Global CISO, I had to adjust based on the business changes NTTS was experiencing while reducing cost and delivering the internal security support as outlined in the ISMS. The strategy and concepts defined in our ISMS did not fundamentally change, and the business outcomes were still valid; however, the delivery philosophy was very different and the impact to our regions was huge.

I continued to travel to each of these areas to ensure that the transitions were going according to plan and that we were executing on schedule. As my contacts in various

> **Lesson Learned:**
> *Try and do what is best for the client – they always remember.*

countries grew, and as I visited clients across the globe, it was clear that they were becoming concerned about NTT Security and its ability to deliver services.

In the Americas, this was much more obvious as competition continued to gain more market share and clients were moving away from our services. In my capacity as a CISO, I listened to our clients and their concerns. I passed them along to the executive team, and important decisions on how to address the issues started to take shape.

As we approached the end of our second quarter, it was clear that we had a lot of work to do. Not only did our transformation require more effort before it could fully be realized, but we had to continue conducting our business-as-usual operations and the employees had to be energized to support the transformation.

There had been two years of continuous change, and there was still more to come – communication had to improve.

Chapter 8: CEO Was Never on the Bucket List

More Challenges

Managing Up

Employees, for the most part, expect to take direction from their managers. However, any employee or manager who works for a boss who is generally disorganized, or whose plate is overfilled, can tell you that it is extremely difficult for the employee to determine what the expectations actually are. This can even extend to specific job responsibility delegation, especially if there is a lack of communication and if the boss is not listening.

If you are like me, enduring uncertainty and doubt is not in the cards. You have another option, "managing up," a concept that has received a lot of attention by various think tanks and analysts over the last few years. Managing up means taking whatever steps necessary to make your boss's job easier. Simply put, you manage the manager.

Yes, it takes a bit of extra time on your part; however, the results may surprise you, and your job will certainly become a little bit easier.

According to Justin Reynolds at TINYPulse, there are several factors that go into managing up. His August 1, 2019, article, "What Does It Mean to Manage Up?" addresses many of these factors, including:

- *Communicating your priority and seeking feedback – Establish a two-way communication*
- *Being able to anticipate your boss's needs – be proactive versus reactive*
- *Understanding what makes your boss tick – get to know the person*
- *Knowing the right way to discuss problems with your boss – know what buttons to push and which ones not to push*
- *Learning how to be a well-rounded source of help – establish a trust relationship and become that trusted advisor*

> **Lesson Learned:**
> *If you disagree with a solution or business outcome, take your boss aside and provide them with an alternative view.*

By conducting yourself with a can-do attitude and in a professional manner, managing up is generally appreciated and usually makes your job more enjoyable. For best results, though, you must balance the yes-man persona with managing up. Good leaders accept constructive criticism from all sources. They listen, assess the information they've received, determine an action in response, and execute it.

Whenever you are in a group of people, never register a vocal disagreement during a gathering of the leader's peers but do approach the leader privately. This is always appreciated. This idea becomes more complicated in a matrixed environment where an employee may have multiple bosses, each with specific direction, and one of the most difficult tasks becomes deciding which boss gets priority and which deserves loyalty.

Managing up using a combination of the

above strategies helps in achieving the objectives of each manager, and your objectives as well, thus removing most of the difficulties created by matrix management.

Another Open Door

As I interacted with staff and employees during the course of my normal workload, I saw the growing anxiety in the people as changes appeared daily. To them, it felt like change for changes' sake; after all, leadership wasn't forthcoming with any real explanations or information.

Every leader has the embedded responsibility to motivate the employee base and generate enthusiasm. I admit I fell a bit short in this arena, especially considering that my focus was on protecting the business (people and assets). I carried the employees' message back to the executive leadership team, first through a conference call, then face to face in Tokyo at a normal meeting of the Executive Leadership Team during the last week in August 2018.

After I completed my presentation, I was asked by the CTO to stop by his office for a short discussion and was asked to meet with the COO. In the last chapter, one of the lessons learned was that "when a door is opened, you must be prepared to walk through it – but do so with open eyes and reasonable expectations," well, it applies here.

During these two meetings, I was asked if I would consider taking the role of Chief Executive Officer (CEO) for NTT Security

Americas. I admit I was somewhat shocked at the time, but I soon overcame the amazement.

"I need to see a detailed offer and discuss compensation," was my answer.

This didn't faze the CTO. The COO was more forthcoming with details, including what he anticipated would be the goals and objectives of the assignment.

The COO explained that the assignment would be for about a year, given the transformation of NTT globally. I would report to him with a matrix line to the Global CEO, and I was to lead the region to profitability.

It was an interesting set of expectations, but I still didn't understand why they pulled me for the job. I asked the COO, and he told me that I had shown the business acumen at the executive team meetings, I had the respect of the employees, and I was connected to the clients and their needs. As I listened, I wondered why they didn't choose a finance person or operations person. Surely, someone like that would be a better fit.

Regardless, I gave the CTO and COO the same response: I wanted to see the details of the goals and objectives and the compensation model. I flew back to the United States on a Friday, and by the time I landed, I had already received an email from the COO with a draft offer letter.

It was unbelievable! I certainly wasn't expecting such a quick response, which started me worrying about what I might be walking into. On Saturday (after a good night's sleep), I reviewed the offer letter and made some necessary corrections that my many mentors had suggested I focus on if I ever went into compensation negotiations. That advice proved to be invaluable.

For those who might be heading in the same direction, I encourage you to check this article out. The graphic is of help, and the article has additional good pointers. (https://www.ceoupdate.com/articles/ceo-pay-categories)

Saturday evening, I received a second draft. Almost everything I had asked for or made changes to was accepted. There was one item that required board sanction, but I didn't want to hold up the final offer letter to wait for that decision. On Sunday, the final offer letter came through. I accepted it as soon as my lawyer was able to review it.

On Monday, I flew to Dallas for an executive meeting with CEOs from around the NTT Businesses in the Americas. There, it was formally announced that I would be the new CEO of NTT Security Americas, effective September 11, 2018. All of this had happened in just four hectic days over a weekend. It was incredible!

Goals and Objectives that Are Clearly Articulated

Goals and objectives at this level, including what I looked for in the offer letter, can be complicated. I can't disclose the contents of my agreement, but I will provide what has been disclosed publicly.

First, I had always been aware that this position would be somewhat temporary in nature given the transformation of NTT.

Since this was my first CEO assignment, I felt it necessary to be transparent with the staff and the direction that I was planning to move the region in and what the focus would be.

These were the top three strategic objectives that I created and received agreement on at that time:

- *Stabilizing the workforce*
- *Stabilizing existing clients*
- *Creating new revenue streams*

There were a lot of moving parts that I had to deal with organizationally, strategically, and with marketing, service delivery, and similar areas.

Stabilizing the workforce and the existing client base were the top priorities. This required a lot of travel, first to hold town halls with the employees and then to meet with clients (especially those that were close to renewal). At one point these goals became so critical that I made these points publicly in the press interviews. In my mind, personal interaction was the only way to ensure both items got the attention they deserved.

People are the core component of our business. Security is a trust business and a people business – fundamentally, it is about the relationships, both at a sales level and a technical expertise level. If you lack either one of those in a business like this, it will fail.

For example, a security executive outsourcing a component of his operations to a third-party service provider needs to have trust in the company and the team providing the services. The executive must also view the relationship with the sales/delivery team as a solid one built from mutual respect and understanding.

Becoming a trusted advisor to a security executive is also crucial to building a business. In the cybersecurity community, word travels fast. If you don't have solid relationships at the security executive level, the reputation of your company will be damaged. Because of this, I was visiting three to five clients per week across the Americas.

Where it made sense geographically, I had my team set up meetings back to back to get the most out of a travel week. Where I could present at conferences, I did, and while at a conference talked with hundreds of potential clients along the way.

In my view, this is what is required for a CEO to support the sales team. People would disagree, or would not spend that kind of time, but I think it proved valuable as renewals began to stabilize, and we saw a measurable increase in new clients. Stabilizing the workforce and the client base became goals that were linked together. Both required over communication to ensure transparency and to drive the best possible business outcomes.

From an employee perspective, I need to provide usable information. I solved this with quarterly formal town hall meetings including presentations by my direct reports, details regarding where the business metrics were and how that impacted each of the employees. I also felt strongly that I needed to do more than that, so after poling a few employees across the Americas region, I started having conference calls (the frequency of which was determined by events that impacted the employees) with the sole purpose of communicating information.

There was no presentation; I simply addressed issues, passed information, discussed challenges, and provided leadership guidance. Feedback from these calls was overwhelmingly positive, and employees felt connected.

Know What You Are Worth

I know everyone reading is waiting for the part where I discuss compensation. Unfortunately, those details of the agreement cannot be disclosed.

However, I think it is safe to encourage each of you to consider what a total compensation package means in today's world. Although the terms of an offer letter are confidential, you can find general information from plenty of reputable sources when you're ready to negotiate your own package.

You must look beyond salary, although that is certainly a big piece of the offer. If you are driven, bonuses tied to performance and metrics based on the goals and objectives you've agreed to should be your focus.

Depending on the company, everything should be on the table, including providing transportation, such as a car, a corporate apartment, vacation (even though you probably won't take it) stock (or preferred stock), membership in various clubs or organizations that would enhance your ability to build relationships, and similar items. These are critical discussion points as you reach the CEO level.

Don't shortchange yourself by not asking questions.

The Puzzle Pieces

I had to make some changes in the organization as I adjusted the overall strategy. Changes in staff, including replacing staff with new blood from outside the organization, while shoring up the perceptions of the employee base, were the most important moves I made.

Here is where a portion of two previous lessons learned became applicable. Remember: "People make teams work – they are like puzzle pieces; you must find the right pieces that form the perfect picture. The more you know and understand your leaders, the better you can fit the pieces together," and "you are served better with people who understand your work ethic and your philosophies."

These lessons became vital as I looked to the outside for individuals who had strengths that would complement my existing team members. My goal, as always, was to create a cohesive team that would be focused on reaching our goals and exceeding expectations. I believe we had created such a team by March 2019, as we headed into a new fiscal year.

Culture and diversity are challenges I have addressed many times in these pages. In a multinational business environment, the American way is not the only path, nor is it always the desired path. The same applies to my British colleagues. As a leader, you must be able to look beyond your own experiences and listen to your team. Their recommendations and observations are crafted by the cultures in which they were raised – in a world economy, those views are critical to understand.

Listen to the individual points of view; they may surprise you, and you may change your entire strategy because of the input from someone who is from another country, culture, or background. Cultural diversity should not be a buzzword but rather a part of the daily operations of a corporation.

No one person has all the answers, but the more input you gather, the more informed your decision will be. However, don't use the act of collecting ideas as a crutch to *not* make a decision. Remember, indecision is really a decision, and every employee will see that.

The Picture

For the first six months of my tenure as CEO for the Americas, I felt like things were turning around. I had a new Chief of Staff, VP of Consulting, Director of Finance, and a direct sales team. Combining these people with a terrific human resources team, a seasoned service delivery team, a tested alliance team, and a stellar technical and security operations team made it seem like things were beginning to gel. The turnaround became more visible, and the numbers continued to drive in the positive direction.

Numbers are never the whole story, though. One of the things I believed I was seeing was that the individual employees were more enthusiastic and appeared to be feeling good. There was a bit less strain on them as we continued executing our strategy. At the sixth-month mark, I asked HR to conduct a survey of the employees to get their anonymous rating of my performance. This would prove definitively whether or not my gut was right.

Caution: if you are a leader, you need to be very comfortable in your own shoes and expect negative feedback. I try to look at the negative feedback as constructive criticism and use it as input to do a better job. Although almost all the feedback from that survey was positive (97%), there were a couple of comments that I took to heart as constructive criticism.

So many things in life and work are situationally dependent, but when you receive negatives, I believe you must address those items.

Lesson Learned:
Always seek feedback from team members and employees; it is the most valuable source of assessment that you can receive.

One comment indicated that the person felt like they were being treated as a shareholder, which I initially thought was odd. But I went back and reviewed all my communications, and there was some truth to the criticism. In my mind, though, every employee was a shareholder of a sort and wanted the company to do well and make a positive return on the investments made. That said, I made a note to review my communications to ensure they were not overly shareholder-centric, unless, of course, I found myself in an employee-owned company where every employee truly is a shareholder.

The second comment was that I tended to be too militaristic. This comment was much more difficult to address than the first. After all, it's very hard to change twenty years of training and cultural indoctrination, although I believe I have done a decent job in making changes so that those who work with me don't feel like they're being addressed in an overly disciplinarian manner.

I continue to review my communications to ensure that I am adjusting as necessary to give the right message to the employees. Just as feedback from the employees was crucial, so was the feedback from the clients. This confidential feedback provided the team insight into how our services were being received and how we might need to make adjustments to ensure a complete and value-added experience was delivered to each of our customers.

From a performance perspective, the executive team was firing on all cylinders: increasing client satisfaction, increasing revenue (quarter over quarter), and delivering solutions at an increased rate. By March 2019, the Americas region had improved significantly and met the goals established in September 2018 by stabilizing the workforce, stabilizing the existing client base, and creating new revenue streams. By July 2019, the new team was exceeding expectations and delivering value.

Continuing the Journey

At the time of this writing, my time as CEO is coming to an end as NTT continues its transformation and the organizational structure is refined. There were six philosophical statements made and one belief that tied things together. There were ten life lessons identified and forty-one lessons learned, which is about one per year of my work history. My hope is that the reader applies the lessons learned to their leadership journey and truly uses this as a learning aid.

As for me, I will move to a new role at the NTT Holdings company level, where I hope to have an impact on future leaders around the globe.

Leadership Lessons Over 40 Years

Chapter 1:

Philosophical Statement Number One: You must be responsible and accountable for your decisions.

Philosophical Statement Number Two: You are never the sharpest tool in the shed – there is always someone smarter.

Philosophical Statement Number Three: Always look to your elders for sage advice. Most of the time they have already been there, done that, and talks like that can save you a lot of time and provide a lot of good information.

Philosophical Statement Number Four: Consider all views, and weigh them accordingly, then own the decision.

Philosophical Statement Number Five: There is always something worthwhile about a person; it is your job to find it.

Life Lesson: Getting married at 18 was not such a good idea.

Life Lesson: Stay away from gambling.

Life Lesson: Two is better than one, but both must realize what life in the military is really like.

Lesson Learned: Control your emotions and do not react to the moment – think through your decision.

Lesson Learned: Identify shortcomings and try to improve them, but also build teams that rely on each other's strengths to counteract individual weaknesses.

Lesson Learned: You can make a mistake – just don't make the same mistake twice.

Lesson Learned: Be leery of the Press – they generally have their own agenda, and it is not helpful to your situation.

Life Lesson: Leaders are forged from the most unexpected sources; you just need to look at the signs.

Philosophical Statement Number Six: Leaders must check their emotions at the door – decisions must be made based on facts, and knee-jerk reactions never end well.

Chapter 2:

Lesson Learned: The ability to put information in compartments and have it at your fingertips when needed is useful, but understanding its value is essential.

Philosophical Beliefs (apply to both military and civilian worlds): He (General Alfred Gray) summarized the core of leadership – civilian or military: "If you come and join my Marines, I want you to know that your number one job is to take care of the men and women you are privileged to lead."

Lesson Learned: Indecision is a decision regardless of the situation.

Lesson Learned: Never believe what the Press reports; their reports are generally wrong and certainly biased, and the best-case scenario is that the reports have small pieces of the truth.

Life Lesson: As a leader, you must deal in facts and take a fact-based approach to all situations, especially the decision-making process.

Life Lesson: As best you can, keep work at work. When you can spend time with the family, be there with the family – really be there.

Lesson Learned: Always study your leaders and glean the best traits and qualities from them.

Lesson Learned: Knowledge is power.

Life Lesson: Try never to burn bridges with people even if there is some pain involved, because you never know when you will meet them again.

Life Lesson: Take time to disconnect from your daily tasks and routine, make time to reenergize and refocus on things that drive your personal needs, and learn to take this time as you need it.

Lesson Learned: From a personal perspective, you must decide how you should operate based on your own personality traits. Know yourself.

Life Lesson: Always be willing to make the tough decisions, that is best for you and your family, and make sure a job is fun – when it stops being fun, it ceases to be a job and becomes a burden.

Chapter 3:

Lesson Learned: Do not allow an employer to use a secondary source of income to justify a lower salary for a current position – it is just not right.

Lesson Learned: *Planning is essential in everything you do, and especially when your own career is at stake. Do not short-change yourself.*

Lesson Learned: *Take the time to understand your customers' needs and desires, not just requirements but what is important (or even critical) to them.*

Lesson Learned: *Sometimes it is necessary to prove the negative.*

Lesson Learned: *Managing human capital is not the same as leading people.*

Lesson Learned: *Listening to people is an art, not a science, and to be successful you must be able to listen.*

Lesson Learned: *Lead by example – ensure that you are doing the same things, following the same processes, or executing on the same values that you are telling, directing, or suggesting the employees must follow, execute, or implement.*

Lesson Learned: *Continually evaluate your leadership capabilities and adjust when needed.*

Lesson Learned: *Listen to the client, understand their needs (requirements), and determine what business outcome they are looking for.*

Chapter 4:

Lesson Learned: *Make a concerted effort to understand your direct reports, both professionally and personally – it will pay dividends down the road.*

Lesson Learned: *Not everyone wants to be a leader, but everyone has some of the leadership traits inside of them.*

Lesson Learned: *Don't focus on the next shiny object without understanding what makes it shine. It is never greener grass on the other side of the mountain.*

Lesson Learned: *Always try to turn a negative situation into a positive situation.*

Lesson Learned: *Don't throw the baby out with the bath water. Everyone has potential and can contribute; you as a leader must figure out what those skills are, highlight them, and mentor each person to be better.*

Lesson Learned: *You never know when a chance meeting becomes an incredible opportunity – always be prepared.*

Lesson Learned: *Cultural diversity is a great thing that can be a game changer and part of the value statement for the company.*

Chapter 5:

Lesson Learned: You can speak your mind and provide honest and accurate (unfiltered) advice or recommendations, and you can walk away from a job if you do not agree with the company's direction or strategy.

Lesson Learned: Automate support functions as much as possible but continue the human interaction.

Lesson Learned: In order to be competitive for any job, you first must be on that hiring manager's list, the boss's list, or the recruiter's list to even be considered.

Chapter 6:

Lesson Learned: When presenting or briefing a board, you must do your homework and understand where each member of the board's background is relating to security, as well as where you may need to focus additional time for an individual member to understand the topic.

Lesson Learned: Do not be afraid to provide criticism and thoughts to individual leaders if they are constructive.

Lesson Learned: Always have a plan B and C ready to go. If the worst-case scenario happens and there's a reduction in force or a cadre of people get fired, you will already have a plan in place to execute if needed.

Lesson Learned: Crisp communication is essential to manage change and employee expectations; if change is occurring all around them, employees will come to various conclusions on their own.

Chapter 7:

Lesson Learned: When a door is opened, you must be prepared to walk through it – but do so with open eyes and reasonable expectations.

Lesson Learned: Where possible, bring former employees who are trustworthy and loyal to work for you. You are served better with people who understand your work ethic and your philosophies.

Lesson Learned: Always execute a termination yourself. Don't staff it out, don't let a human resources person handle it, don't do it by phone. Conduct the termination of a person yourself, in person, and be prepared to provide an explanation. Certainly, you should have an HR person in the room to support you, and perhaps a legal person depending on the circumstances, but you must take ownership of the decision.

Life Lesson: People make teams work – they are like puzzle pieces; you must find the right pieces that form the perfect picture. The more you know and understand your leaders, the better you can fit the pieces together.

Lesson Learned: Things are not chiseled in stone – you can change direction. You must lead change and manage the expectation of change.

Lesson Learned: Do your best to do the right thing every time. This expands on several previous lessons that I have learned over the years, and sometimes the right thing is not the most popular thing.

Lesson Learned: Try and do what is best for the client – they always remember.

Chapter 8:

Lesson Learned: If you disagree with a solution or business outcome, take your boss aside and provide them with an alternative view.

Lesson Learned: Always seek feedback from team members and employees; it is the most valuable source of assessment that you can receive.

www.ingramcontent.com/pod-product-compliance
Lightning Source LLC
Chambersburg PA
CBHW042334150426
43194CB00005B/157